the Christmas House

the *Christmas House*

*How One Man's Dream Changed
the Way We Celebrate Christmas*

GEORJA SKINNER

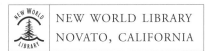

NEW WORLD LIBRARY
NOVATO, CALIFORNIA

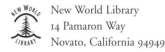

New World Library
14 Pamaron Way
Novato, California 94949

Edited by Eric Bolt
Cover and text design by Mary Ann Casler

Library of Congress Cataloging-in-Publication Data
Skinner, Georja.
The Christmas house : how one man's dream changed the way we celebrate Christmas / By Georja Skinner.
     p.   cm.
ISBN 1-57731-474-3 (hardcover : alk. paper)
1. Christmas—California—Los Angeles. 2. Christmas decorations—California—Los Angeles. 3. Los Angeles (Calif.)—Social life and customs. 4. Skinner, George, d. 1978. I. Title.
GT4986.C2S55 2005
394.2663—dc22   2005007428

First printing, October, 2005
ISBN 1-57731-474-3
ISBN-13 978-1-57731-474-5

New World Library is dedicated to preserving the earth and its resources. We are now printing 50% of our new titles on 100% chlorine-free postconsumer waste recycled paper. As members of the Green Press Initiative (www.greenpressinitiative.org), our goal is to use 100% recycled paper for all of our titles by 2007.

Distributed by Publishers Group West
Printed in China

10   9   8   7   6   5   4   3   2   1

For Mom and Dad,
my sister, Teresa,
Gordon and Walter,
Albert and especially Alice.

And to all those who still believe in impossible dreams.

Contents

A Word from the Director of Warm Springs

It is my pleasure and duty to suggest to you that *The Christmas House* is as large a story as that told of Franklin Delano Roosevelt's fight to be cured of a seemingly unbeatable disease. This is a story of yet another human being, George Skinner, of great courage and caring whose net life product impacted so many of a generation that changed the world. Thank you for adding your father's life to the annals of history. In this time of false heroes, we must be reminded that there are true heroes in our midst. They are often silent, yet they have gifts to offer humanity.

Kenneth R. Harris Sr.
Director of Roosevelt Warm Springs
Development Fund, Inc.
Warm Springs, Georgia
March 14, 2005

Prologue ~ A Christmas Legacy

From as far back as I can remember, Christmas was a magical time around the Skinner household, and the magic extended beyond the usual festivities and anticipation of the season. The holiday held special meaning for my parents and grandfather, and I cherish my childhood memories of Christmas. I vividly remember my sister, Teresa, Dad, and I finishing our door-to-door candy cane deliveries. Christmas music blared from the battery-powered tape player and speaker we pulled along in our red wagon as we made our rounds. I remember hiding just inside our bedroom door, waiting for Mom to call out, "I think Santa stopped by last night. There are lots of presents here for someone special." On Christmas mornings we would make a beeline for the stockings hanging from the fireplace mantel.

We lived in the flats of Hollywood, a blue-collar area, and money was tight. So by necessity Christmas presents in the Skinner family served more as symbols of love and appreciation than pacifiers of materialistic cravings. It really didn't matter what was given as long as the gift was heartfelt and expressed the personality of the giver and recipient. In fact, it seemed the best gifts were the smallest and least expensive, like the handmade toys that lasted all year or the stuffed owl

Georja Skinner in sleigh, Curson Avenue, 1953

my sister owns to this day. Humorous gifts, such as socks with no openings and exploding cigars, also scored high marks in our household. This liberating attitude allowed us to come up with clever and unexpected tokens of our love for one another year after year.

Our celebration of Christmas was unique in another way. When it came to the tradition of decorating, the Skinner family Christmas was a bit like a Hollywood production, albeit on a shoestring budget. Indeed, growing up at our house was like living at Disneyland, with Dad planning for Christmas all year long. Even in July, we had "snow" because our front lawn was replaced with thousands of white rocks. My mother teased Granddad that he had been drunk when he put up our white

George and daughter Georja with Santa in front of Curson Avenue home, 1953

picket fence, which was erratic and crooked so it would look like a fence built by elves. And we had an outdoor fireplace where fake logs glowed all night to "warm" anyone walking by.

My father turned the decoration of the home at the holidays into a new art form, and many people credit him with launching the holiday decorating tradition that is still practiced today. Thank George Skinner when you see houses covered with strings of multicolored lights and roofs topped with fake snow and Rudolph the Red-Nosed Reindeer towing Santa Claus in his sleigh.

My father was passionate about Christmas. He believed Christmas was the perfect time to celebrate all the joy that comes with living, and he did his best to spread good cheer. And what better way to express his holiday spirit than through the elaborate embellishment of his house with icons of Christmas for all to appreciate? As far as he was concerned, everyone had something to celebrate, be it family, friends, good health, or two nickels to rub together.

His zeal came from an unlikely place: the polio epidemic of 1934. After a nearly fatal bout with the illness in his early twenties, my father realized that those who have hit rock bottom can benefit from a liberal dose of Christmas spirit. Many people who have had a near-death experience speak of seeing a bright white light, often at the end of a tunnel. However, when George almost died, he saw something quite different, and he saw it for weeks on end as he drifted between life and death. Instead of a white light, he saw lit-up Christmas trees, houses covered in snow, and images of the childhood home he had left behind in Canada. He took this as divine intervention and vowed that if he survived he would share his vision of Christmas with as many people as possible.

When I was seven years old, my father shared his vision with me by giving me the Christmas gift I remember best. I can vividly recall how he watched as I opened a small, flat package, a package that contained an old postcard with a photograph of a tiny house decorated for the holidays. The house in the picture was the house my father and grandfather lived in long before I was born, in the Boyle Heights district of Los Angeles. It was where he realized his dream of the Christmas House. The story of that house is told in the pages of this book, and it's a testament to what my father told me on that Christmas when I was seven: "If you believe, even your wildest dreams are possible."

George Skinner outside the original Christmas House, Mathews Street, Boyle Heights, Los Angeles, 1936

~

My own appreciation for Christmas waned shortly after my father passed away in 1978. After his death the holiday season wasn't a time I looked forward to, despite my family's legacy of holiday enthusiasm. The over-commercialization of Christmas left me wondering if my father's vision of goodwill really mattered anymore. The true meaning of Christmas seemed lost, as advertisers jump-started the shopping season earlier every year, enticing us to dash to the malls for rampant buying. Hearing things like "only three shopping days left until Christmas" sent pangs of frustration through my body. All the holiday hype wasn't about spending quality time with family and friends but about merchants and merchandise and families racking up huge credit card debt. Neighbors competed to see who could have the most elaborate holiday decorations, hiring professionals to put on the spectacular shows rather than doing it themselves.

I came to think that Scrooge's attitude toward Christmas had some merit. Instead of halls decked with boughs of holly and visions of sugar plums dancing in my head, I saw mindless frenzy, congested airports, inconsiderate drivers, no parking spaces, and gifts that didn't "keep on giving." I had completely lost touch with the spirit that my father brought to Christmas.

It wasn't until 1997, when my sister and I were closing out our parents' estate after our mother passed away, that we rediscovered the Skinner Christmas legacy. We were sorting through our parents' possessions at the last home we all shared in Hollywood. Since my parents and grandfather had been consummate pack rats and my sister and I lived three thousand miles away on the island of Maui, the task was daunting. They had saved every check stub, utility bill, photograph, and scrap of paper remotely connected to the Skinner household. What qualified as family memorabilia and what went to the Salvation

Sisters Georja and Teresa on Christmas Day in Curson Avenue living room, 1963

Army often came down to a coin toss. We considered stopping many times, overwhelmed by both the amount of work left to do and the loss we felt.

Then, in the midst of the chaos we discovered in the hall closet my father's most cherished possession. Neatly packed inside a cake box from a bakery long since out of business was a large wood-bound scrapbook that I hadn't seen since I was a teenager. As my sister and I slowly turned the pages, we felt as though we were in a time warp. The entire afternoon passed as we pored over the photographs and read the letters contained within. The items in the scrapbook told the story of how our father had turned into reality his dream of what Christmastime was meant to be. In fact, this very book you

Cover of wooden scrapbook belonging to George Skinner

are holding is largely based on what was pasted onto and stuck between the pages of that scrapbook.

Since I rediscovered this treasure, my faith in Christmas has been reborn. Amazingly, I now ignore the bombardment of advertisements with their prescribed gift suggestions and shopping deadlines. Instead, I recall the atmosphere my father created when I was a child. I enthusiastically revel in holiday festivities as he would have wanted, sharing goodwill with family members, friends, and strangers.

The story of George Skinner's Christmas House takes us back to a less complicated time. His gift to a community transformed the holiday for thousands, igniting joy and camaraderie and healing at least one life in the process — his own.

the Christmas House

Chapter 1 ~ Prisoner of Polio

The year 1934 started off with a bang for twenty-two-year-old George Skinner. He was living in Los Angeles with his father, Albert. He and his father were close, and they stayed active, taking camping trips and swimming at the beach regularly. Though he often thought longingly of his mother and brothers — left behind in Canada fourteen years before — he was enjoying life. Going to college and having a steady girlfriend took up most of his time. As his year of studies wound down, he expected to receive his business diploma soon, and he was thinking it was time to get serious about his life. What type of job would he have when he finished school? Should he pop the question to his girlfriend, Allison?

His life took another tack, however. George was stricken with polio while swimming laps at the Los Angeles City College pool on May 22, while his girlfriend was reading a book poolside. A minute or two went by before Allison realized how quiet

Left: George playing stickball on Venice Beach, 1921
Above: George's first camping trip to a California Beach with his father, Albert, 1920

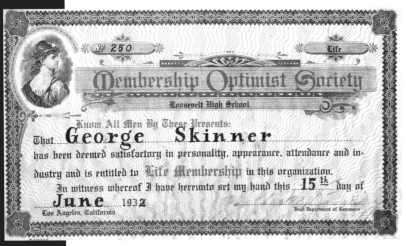

Life membership certificate from the Optimist Society, 1932

it was. She didn't hear the familiar sound of George paddling and kicking as he racked up his usual twenty laps per day. She lowered her book and looked up, but he was nowhere to be seen, and the surface of the water was mysteriously as smooth as glass. When she stood up she saw him underwater, slowly sinking to the bottom of the pool. His arms and legs were spread-eagle and motionless, but his eyes were wide open. At first, Allison thought it was a prank, and she waved for him to rise to the surface, but he sank to the bottom of the eight-foot-deep pool.

"No one can hold his breath that long, not even fit-as-a-fiddle George," she realized. Suddenly, she knew

this was no joke and screamed for help. Two athletes arrived from the men's locker room and pulled George's nearly lifeless body to the surface. He was still breathing, but barely. As his mind floated in and out of consciousness, his body was loaded into an ambulance and, with the siren screaming all the way, rushed to the emergency room at Los Angeles County General Hospital.

The doctor immediately recognized that George had symptoms characteristic of poliomyelitis, which include the partial or complete paralysis of limbs and vital organs. George's father, Albert, was then summoned to the hospital. The doctor told Albert that the poliovirus destroys the neurons of the spinal cord and brain stem, often without warning, and that this paralysis could result in death. While the doctor talked to him,

George and two friends in beach togs, Santa Monica, 1933

Albert recalled an episode that George had had two months before, when he had collapsed and the doctor he saw diagnosed a spinal problem and administered an injection. At that time, no one had mentioned the possibility of polio.

There was no known cure for the virus and no way to prevent it. The only treatment at the time was isolation, rest, and morphine to relieve the pain. Essentially, the polio patient's own immune system was the only defense against the disease. The severity and extent of the damage caused by polio covered the entire gamut. Some patients recovered quickly with no side effects,

Alice Skinner, Joe Palmer with pipe, Walter Skinner, Lily Skinner, George Skinner, and other family members, 1916

Aunt Lily with nephews George, Gordon, and Walter, near Hamilton, Ontario, 1918

George and Walter shovel snow on the front porch steps, 1916

Aunt Lily keeps an eye on the Skinner boys, 1917

others were left paralyzed for life, and across the country, thousands succumbed. At the time George was admitted, Los Angeles County General Hospital was filled to capacity, and they treated 2,500 cases of polio between May and November of 1934.

Patients who could not breathe on their own because of the paralysis had to be put inside what was called an iron lung, an airtight steel-and-glass chamber that reduces the air pressure around the chest cavity. The reduced air pressure allowed patients to expand and contract their lungs more freely. George's preliminary diagnosis of poliomyelitis was confirmed through blood tests. His symptoms were so severe the doctor took Albert aside to deliver the bad news. "Your son must immediately be placed in an iron lung because he isn't able to breathe on his own. And if some lung function isn't regained, he probably won't last a week. Even if he survives, he may never walk again because his spine and the nerves controlling his legs are severely damaged. Basically, at this

George photographed by his father at Los Angeles County General Hospital, 1934

point, his brain is unable to communicate with his lower extremities."

Albert followed George's gurney into the polio ward, where dozens of patients were lying inside iron lungs that resembled caskets with small viewing windows. These extremely noisy contraptions creaked and groaned as they pumped oxygen into the chamber. Locked inside of an iron lung, the only thing George could see was the ceiling. Normally, a mirror was attached so patients could see their surroundings reflected in the glass, but the hospital had been inundated with polio victims and mirrors were at a premium. It would take several weeks before George would get one.

After they arrived in the polio ward, the doctor told George the disease had spread through 80 percent of his body and there was a strong possibility that he would never walk again. George heard everything the doctor told him and his father about his condition and the possible consequences. He wasn't able to speak and could only blink his eyes in acknowledgment. The shock silenced Albert, usually a talkative and happy-go-lucky man. Neither he nor George had been prepared for this sudden, tragic change of plans, and they were too stunned to do more than listen quietly. Eventually, Albert was asked to leave since the polio ward was under strict quarantine.

In spite of a raging fever and intense pain, George later recalled much of his first night in the hospital. Although at the time he was drifting in and out of consciousness and could not even speak to his father or the nurses who tried to comfort him, he later wrote down his fearful memories of the experience:

My body wouldn't respond. I couldn't move anything no matter how hard I tried. It was like my arms and legs weren't connected to me. I felt like my brain was in another place, as my body lay trapped in steel.

I asked myself, why me? I believe in God; I go to church. One minute I'm playing varsity sports, the president of the Optimist Society, in love with Allison, and then suddenly I'm paralyzed, on the verge of death.

Lying awake that night, George accepted the fact that he may not survive, and if he did, he may spend the rest of his life as a paraplegic or quadriplegic. If a major handicap or death was the route God had chosen for him, so be it, but he wasn't about to go without a fight. While locked inside the hissing, vibrating

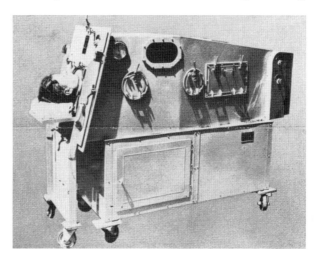

Polio patient in iron lung, 1933

machine, he pictured his lungs inflating and deflating. Each attempted breath, no matter how weak, was a form of meditation to George.

The chapters of George's short life passed before his eyes as he lay there. One unresolved issue kept cropping up: what had become of his mother and

George (right) and his younger brother, Walter, play in the snow in Hamilton, Ontario, 1916

brothers in Canada? He vividly recalled the cold night when he was seven years old and his father woke him up to take him on a train trip. What was supposed to be an overnighter lasted weeks, all the way from Hamilton, Ontario, to Los Angeles. His father had called that trip an extended vacation. George trusted his father and made the best of his new life in Southern California. A year later, Albert told him they probably would never return to Canada because the winters wreaked havoc on George's health. It had now been fourteen years.

If George was going to die, he wanted to die knowing the truth about their departure from Canada in January 1920. The stories his father told him were too pat, as if they were well rehearsed. They didn't explain why his mother, Alice, and his two brothers, Walter and Gordon, were left behind. Couldn't they have all moved together like a normal family? And why were there no letters or phone calls from them, or from anybody back home? Whenever the subject of family was mentioned, especially at birthdays and holidays, Albert refused to talk about it and quickly changed the subject. Finally, when George was thirteen, he stubbornly quizzed his father about his mother and brothers. Albert choked up and told him his mother was dead and his brothers' whereabouts were unknown. Lying in his hospital bed contemplating his survival, George replayed those cherished memories of growing up in Canada. He thought about the snowball fights with his brothers, decorating the Christmas tree with mom and dad, and hiking in the woods. He wished there was some way to have his family back with him. If only they could all be together again.

George and Walter playing on the icy banks of Lake Ontario, Canada, 1917

George's brother Gordon with their mother, Alice, in the kitchen on Lottridge Street, Hamiltion, 1919

Chapter 2 ~ A Father's Love, a Mother's Loss

For the next several months, George underwent daily confinement in an iron lung for six hours or more because his lungs were too weak to breathe without mechanical assistance. The iron lung was extremely claustrophobic and tested a patient's will to live. It was not uncommon to hear screams of "Get me out of here — I can't take it anymore!" coming from inside the polio ward. This torturous treatment was followed by intense and painful massage therapy — not the kind found at health spas today with relaxing music and aromatherapy. George's massage and physical therapy consisted of a nurse vigorously stretching and pulling his arms and legs until he writhed in agony. Medical research showed that polio patients who underwent this type of physical therapy regained the use of their limbs more quickly than sedentary patients. George didn't complain about the regimen because he knew from years of athletic activities that muscles and joints quickly atrophy if they're not exercised. The thought of being confined to a wheelchair enabled him to endure the pain. He even teased the nurses about their taking a perverse delight in his painful massage sessions.

Preston Goddard, George's therapist at Los Angeles County General Hospital, 1934

George's entire ward was still under strict quarantine because polio was so contagious; an errant sneeze or cough could easily transmit the virus. NO VISITORS ALLOWED signs were posted everywhere, but somehow Albert managed to charm his way past the nurses every few days to visit his son. He always brought a small gift to lift George's spirits. One day it was a candy bar and the next, homemade cookies, but what really boosted George's spirits were the many get-well cards and letters. George saved and cherished every one he received. He was amazed at how many people cared about his well-being. The cards and letters came from friends, neighbors, and church members. He vowed to himself that he would repay their kindness tenfold if he ever got out of the hospital.

George knew his attitude toward his health might make the difference between being confined to a wheelchair and walking on his own two feet.

Last portrait of the Skinner family together, 1919

Alice Woodcock Skinner, 1915

Aunt Lily dressed as Santa with Gordon and Alice, 1917

Family picnic in Hamilton, Ontario, 1917 (left to right, Alice, Walter, Gordon, George, and Aunt Lily in back)

Picnic with Skinner relatives, 1917

George riding tricycle with playmates on Lottridge Street, Hamilton, 1915

His can-do disposition had helped him many times over the years. When he was a child, it had given him the courage to start a new life in California and never look back. In high school, it had earned him the necessary votes to win the title of student body president. But one unresolved issue was preventing him from fully adopting the positive attitude he needed to win the battle with polio: George couldn't stop thinking about his family in Canada.

He spent many hours lying awake and thinking about his life. He liked to recall memories from his childhood as a way of distracting himself from his pain and discomfort, but the memories always brought his mind back to the question about his relatives who had been left behind. Why hadn't they visited him or at least sent a get-well card? He needed their support and love more than ever. He felt that a connection with them would make all the difference in his recovery. His father had to know more than he was admitting, and the next time Albert visited, George planned to ask him about it. If he didn't answer, George would confront him. He vowed to not let Albert change the subject or gloss over the truth, no matter what.

One day during a massage session, while Albert read get-well cards, George stopped him mid-sentence. "Why aren't there any letters from Canada, not even one from Aunt Lily?" George knew his father still communicated with his sister, Lily. "Surely, she knows of my condition."

George's tone of voice was more determined than ever before, and Albert quickly realized that excuses and changing the subject wouldn't work this time. After a long pause, Albert admitted, "Lily has written. She wishes you well."

George looked sternly at his father and said, "Read one of her letters to me then. Can't you bring them with you when you visit?"

The next day when he arrived, Albert nervously took a bundle of letters from his satchel and opened a letter dated the previous June. Albert began reading the letter silently to himself. Watching this from his bed, George demanded, "Read it out loud, Dad."

The nurse realized the gravity of the situation and left the ward. Albert began reading:

Aunt Lily with Walter, Christmas Day, 1917

Dearest Albert,

It isn't good to dwell on the past, dear brother. Things have gone from bad to worse with your family. I know your intentions were good and you are not to be blamed. Please don't feel bad, for we all make mistakes. Gordon and Walter are now on their own and haven't heard anything from their mother, Alice, in some time. It seems Alice has literally vanished. We don't know where she is.

Poor George. I pray that God will give him the strength to survive this horrible disease. Please give him my love and tell him that we are praying for him.

Your loving sister,
Lily

As he folded the letter to return it to the envelope, Albert's hands were shaking, and tears rolled down his cheeks. George was in shock, trying to make sense of Lily's words and why his father had hidden the fact that his mother was still alive. How could he be so thought-less? Finally, George couldn't withhold his anger and lashed out. "How dare you!" he said. Albert trembled, and his face was pale. George continued, "Why did you lie to me? You told me my mother was dead!"

In the silence that followed, Albert worked to regain enough composure to answer his son. Finally, he said, "I'm sorry, but I had to get you out of Canada. It was too cold up there for your weak constitution. You had whooping cough and repeated bouts of diph-theria." Albert paused and then took a deep breath. "On top of that, I got myself in hot water because I fancied the ladies, and your mother didn't understand. Nothing ever happened, mind you, but she didn't believe me. I dishonored my family and myself. I intended to help your mother once we got settled in California, but when we arrived, I realized it wasn't that easy to make a living here. It was all I could do to keep you and me fed. Then, your aunt Lily wrote me that your mother had told your brothers I had died in the war. Your mother couldn't afford to take care of them herself, so she put them in a home for boys. Believe me, if I knew she was giving them up, I would have done something, but I didn't find out until it was too late. I can't contact them now; I don't know where they are."

Alice, Walter, Lily, and George, 1916

Albert reading in parlor, Hamilton, 1919

George and his mother with playmate, 1916

At that moment, George despised his father and thought about telling him to leave and never come back. But soon he realized that rejecting his father would be equivalent to what his father had done to his family in Canada.

"You took me from my mother and brothers and brought me to Los Angeles for your own selfish reasons. It explains why you flirt with all the nurses and every other woman you meet. You broke Mom's heart and my brothers' hearts, and now you're breaking mine."

In the silence that followed, they both retreated to their own thoughts. Albert hung his head and sobbed. He felt he had lost his son and his best friend. George didn't know what to do next. On the one hand, his father had provided a good life for him, but on the other hand, he had totally deceived him about his family.

After much soul-searching, George struggled to reach out from his bed and touch his father's shoulder. "I know you didn't hurt anyone intentionally, but you

Alice and her firstborn son, George, 1916

Albert's sister, Lily, who stayed in touch through letters, 1919

have to realize that your actions have terrible repercussions. I'll forgive you, Pop, but you have to promise me you'll try to find my brothers and Mom soon. It's really important to me."

Amazed that George could move his arm, Albert took his hand and held it tightly until the nurse appeared in the doorway and told them it was time for iron lung treatments. Albert gave George's hand a squeeze and then departed.

Five days went by with no visits from Albert, leading George to wonder if he too was being abandoned. Christmas was only a week away, and Albert knew that it was George's favorite time of the year.

George playing in his backyard, Hamilton, 1916

The ward wasn't the same without lively Albert around, playing practical jokes and rendering free advice to nurses, doctors, and patients. Just after dark, as the patients were dozing before dinner, George and his ward mates were startled by the sound of someone awkwardly opening a third-story window and entering the polio ward. George said aloud, "Who on earth would want to break into the hospital?"

Many of the men in the ward laughed at George's joke as they waited to see who it was. A man wearing a wrinkled doctor's smock entered the room and hollered, "Merry Christmas." Everyone recognized the intruder's voice as

Walter and George in the park, 1917

Albert's. Somehow, he had managed to climb up the fire escape in the dark with a stuffed pillowcase in one hand and a small Christmas tree in the other.

The sight of Albert made everyone in the ward laugh. Even patients confined in iron lungs got a kick out of Albert, but their laughter quickly turned into coughing fits. A nurse entered to investigate the clamor. When she saw Albert, she playfully covered her ears and said, "I didn't hear a thing," and then quickly exited the room. Albert proceeded to decorate the three-foot pine tree with a string of popcorn and homemade ornaments. Reaching into the pocket of his trousers, he brought out a handkerchief and gently unfolded it, holding up the ornament inside for George to see. It was an old tin star with tiny pieces of mirror glued to it. Spears of light reflected off the star, shooting to the walls and ceiling. Albert brought the ornament closer to George and asked, "Remember this?"

George immediately recognized it as the star his mother had hung over his bed when he was a child. His mother called it the "dreaming star" because when she finished reading a bedtime story, she gave the star a spin to send George and his brothers off to sleep. She said the dreaming star would make their fondest dreams come true.

"I've wanted to give this to you for a long time, Sonny. I know it meant a lot to you when you were younger, and maybe now it will help you get well," Albert said. He hung the star directly over George's bed. The gift touched George, and with it hanging over him, he felt closer to his mother than ever before.

Albert proceeded to don a Santa Claus hat and serve dinner to his son, cutting the pork chop into tiny pieces. "Not too small," George said with a grin. "I'm not a child anymore."

After dinner, Albert pulled a gift out of the pillowcase he had carried with him, a tabletop radio. He held it high for all to see, announcing, "This is for everyone." He plugged the radio into a wall outlet, turned the volume to full, and cocked his head toward the speaker as swing music filled the ward. Patients nodded and turned their heads in their beds as they tried to keep time to the music. The next song on the radio was a new release, "Santa Claus Is Coming to Town," which everyone in the ward did their best to sing along to. When the song was over, George asked Albert where he had gotten the money for the radio, considering they didn't have enough money to make their house payments. Albert said, "The congregation at the Baptist church took up a collection and decided a radio would bring the greatest pleasure to you and your ward mates."

Albert in California, 1934

Later that night, after Albert had left and things quieted down, George gazed at the dreaming star and thought of his mother. Wherever she was living, she probably had the house ready for Christmas, with a beautifully decorated tree with holiday garlands all around. The aroma of freshly baked bread and turkey surely filled the air. He wished she could be at his bedside right now. A nurse walked by and softly said, "Go to sleep, George. That's enough excitement for tonight." He drifted off and dreamed about playing in the snow with his brothers and his mother's smile as she stood on the porch in the wintry cold, watching her boys.

Alice watches her sons play in the snow from her front porch, 1915

Chapter 3 ~ Gifts from Unexpected Places

The doctors and nurses were amazed at George's progress. In the first nine months that he was in the hospital, he went from complete paralysis of his arms and legs to regaining limited mobility of his left arm. He attributed his recovery to his insistence on extra hours of physical therapy and his determination to walk again. However, the medical staff kept George's enthusiasm in check by reminding him that there was little hope of him ever walking out of the hospital. Most likely, they said, George would exit the hospital in a wheelchair, as most acute polio patients did, and he would be lucky if he could get around on crutches or braces for the rest of his life. The staff admired his positive attitude but feared he would be a candidate for major depression if his unrealistic hopes didn't come true.

President Franklin Delano Roosevelt was an inspiration to all the patients in the polio ward at Los Angeles County General Hospital. He was living proof that a polio survivor could not only be a productive member of society but could even become the president of the United States. Roosevelt had lost the use of his legs in his battle with polio, and initially he attempted to hide his disability by shielding himself behind a podium when making speeches. He feared that people would doubt that a paraplegic could effectively lead a country with so many economic and political problems. He was determined never to let this become an obstacle to fulfilling his duties, though many outspoken politicians urged him to step down.

The tabletop radio Albert had provided for the ward at Christmas enabled the patients to listen to Roosevelt's *Fireside Chats,* a weekly radio program in which the president discussed his solutions to the country's problems. Most of his chats dealt with economic and political issues, such as the Public Works Project, but one week Roosevelt devoted an entire speech to his

George's typewritten account of his ordeal with polio, 1936

Albert and George on an excursion to the San Gabriel Mountains, 1922

Walter plays the piano while George sings, 1916

bout with polio. He discussed how he had personally donated time and money to help establish the Georgia Warm Springs Foundation, a hydrotherapy center for polio victims in Warm Springs, Georgia. George and his ward mates listened closely to every word. They felt the president was talking directly to them.

"And then there is the tremendous problem as to what is to be done with those hundreds of thousands already ruined by the after-effects of this affliction. To investigate, to study, to develop every medical possibility of enabling those so afflicted to become economically independent in their local communities will be one of the chief aims of the new foundation," President Roosevelt declared.

He went on to credit the healing waters and hydrotherapy for his recovery and said he routinely received treatments at the Warm Springs facility. The therapy consisted of Roosevelt being lowered into the warm mineral water via a sling or gurney. The water

Walter and George in their coal-box "sleigh," 1915

supported his weight, allowing him to exercise his limbs more freely and with less pain. First Lady Eleanor Roosevelt acknowledged that the therapy had worked wonders on her husband. She highly recommended the treatment to all patients suffering from the debilitating effects of polio.

Of course, George was intrigued with anything that might speed his recovery, and he asked his doctor about the possibility of he and his ward mates receiving this type of treatment. Hospital administrators informed him that he would have to pay an exorbitant fee for the specialized type of therapy practiced at Warm Springs. Hydrotherapy was only offered free of charge to polio victims under the age of eighteen. George didn't think that was fair. He felt essential treatments should be provided to all patients regardless of their age or financial means. He decided that he would do whatever he could to change this policy. George insisted the head nurse provide him with a typist so he could compose a letter to Eleanor Roosevelt. Most patients and staff thought the letter was a waste of time. As much as they admired President Roosevelt and the First Lady, they doubted they would have the time to read a letter from a common citizen like George.

An attractive nurse's aide named Pearl Majoros was assigned the task of taking down George's letter. George vaguely recognized Pearl but couldn't place where he had seen her before. When he asked, she reminded him that she was the nurse's aide who had assisted him a year before when he had first arrived by ambulance. She was pleased by his progress and admired his verve. She gladly acted as a professional secretary and took down the letter in shorthand exactly as George dictated it. In the letter, George outlined his

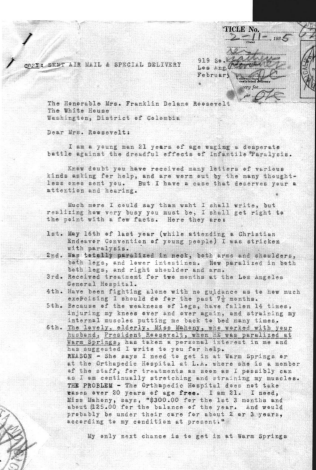

Typewritten letter to Mrs. Roosevelt, 1935

```
                                              #3.
At last I could see friends.
have flowers.. Little gifts.          Thanks to C.E.
Blessing were beging to open up to me.
     THE THRILL TO WALK AGAIN
     THE THRILL OF HAVING MY DAD JOIN TH* CHUCH and be
a partner with me in Cristian Work.
     I now read more than I ever did. I enjoy it.
     Powerful friends.  IWOULD HATE TO LOSE.
I shall always welcome obstacles on Lifes Pathway.  Because
with each obstical you hurdle, the more you get out of life

I thnk Obsticals are an opportuntiy.  The layman and the
Great Men of HIstory, who have got the most joy out of
life have had a hard journy.   They have not trod the
EASY ROAD ON LIFES PATHWAY.  Obstacles & Courage makes
life more beautiful, richer, thrilling, MAKES LIFE MORE
WORTH WHILE.LE*VING FOR.
```

Goals and wishes for his recovery written by George, 1936

history with polio and the circumstances that made it impossible for him or his father to pay for treatment. He mentioned that he had no mother and that his father, though working full-time, could barely keep up with the mortgage payments on their home. He told Mrs. Roosevelt that they were in danger of losing the house to foreclosure. Pearl promised to type the letter word for word, provide George with a carbon copy, and mail it that day.

Pearl and George hit it off quite well, and George asked her for a date. "Once I get out of the hospital, of course," he said with a chuckle. But that hope was quickly dashed when Pearl informed him she was leaving for San Francisco the next day to visit her father. Her family was going through a difficult transition, as her parents had recently separated. As she was leaving, she wished him the best. George didn't let her rejection get him down. He figured a young lady as attractive as she was probably wouldn't be interested in a romance with a handicapped person. He had learned that lesson from Allison; not long after George was hospitalized, she had stopped corresponding with him altogether, and he had heard through mutual friends that she was already dating another man.

George made slow progress over the next two months. Both arms regained some feeling and mobility, though his muscle mass was slow to rebuild. His legs were still completely paralyzed. He appreciated the get-well letters from neighbors and friends but felt he could read between the lines: Many people didn't think he would ever fully recover. One afternoon, he was taken by surprise by the arrival of a letter with a return address of The White House, Washington, District of Columbia. George waited to open it until all the able-bodied patients were gathered around his bed. Then, he dramatically read the letter aloud, as if making a proclamation.

Dear George Skinner,

Please be advised that Mrs. Eleanor Roosevelt has received your letter and is pleased that you have brought this matter to her attention. We understand that Mrs. Mahoney, a nurse who attended to President Roosevelt, is currently residing in Los Angeles, and we have requested that she assist you in your recovery from polio.
She will ensure that you receive similar hydrotherapy as practiced at The Warm Springs Rehabilitation Center. As for the impending foreclosure on your home at Mathews Street, we've referred the matter to a California organization that will be reviewing the matter and will contact you directly.

The First Lady thanks you for bringing this to her attention. Best wishes on your recovery.

Sincerely, assistant to Eleanor Roosevelt

George and his ward mates were ecstatic. They whistled and hollered in jubilant disbelief that the First Lady had responded so powerfully to George's letter.

~

Page 2.

Could not sleep-dope,dope. terribly nervous. Teeth all lose. Hard to eat. Blood tests, injections, needles I CANNOT SEE WHY ALL THIS SHOULD COME TO ME. HAD I NOT TRIED TO GET PEOPLE TO CHURCH AND C. E.? I TRIED TO DO ALL I COULD IN C.E. I TRIED TO LIVE RIGHT. EVERYTHING SEEMED WRONG. God Knows it took Courage Now and lots of it.
All casts come off. Could not sleep in one position over 30min to half hr. Back, all bed sores from laying all this time on wooden frame. Could feel my ribs and bones protruding. Not fat at all. 40 lbs gone. AND YET I HAD TO REMAIN QUIET TO SAVE EVERY BIT OF ENERY I had The doctors didn't seem to know what to do. In fact some said they were groping in the dark.
Got severe cold--Not enough energy to fight it. Gave me eight shots.injections to fight it. Hemorage-could not stop it for half hr. From Canda, Got picture I pinned on cast for right arm that read underneath-He Careth for You. IT GAVE ME MORE COURAGE IN ADDITION TO THE LETTERS FROM MY MANY FIREND.(#25 letter} Icould not understand the WHY of all this. Now I do! It seems God has to be severe sometimes to make us or othe see a thing, that they cannot comprehend unless.

By this time I had been in the Hospital almost 2 monthes. The only thing I could read and understand was letters. I just looked at pictures in magazines. I knew the entire Church and others were standing by me in prayer.
MY FAITH INCREASED AND CONTINUEDF TO INCREASE.

The details of his bout with polio and physical challenges written by George in 1936

Soon after that, on August 19, 1935, fifteen months after nearly drowning in a swimming pool, George was lowered by gurney into the warm waters of a hydrotherapeutic pool similar to the one used by the president of the United States. The restorative powers of the water and the attention of President Roosevelt's private nurse brought swift progress. Within months of receiving these treatments, George gained enough strength in his legs to take small steps with the aid of leg braces and crutches.

After many more months of hydrotherapy in con-junction with physical therapy, Dr. Madsen, his doctor, stood by George's bedside with clipboard in hand. His long pause concerned Albert and George, but he broke it by declaring that George was well enough to go home. It was April 1936. They were elated, and as his son struggled to stand up Albert held him tight in a shaky embrace.

George didn't sleep well his last night in the hospital because he was struck with the notion that he essentially had to reinvent George Skinner. Physically he was a very different person from the one who had

George being lowered into the hydrotherapy pool at Los Angeles County General Hospital, 1935

arrived by ambulance nearly two years before. He knew he'd never regain the strength and coordination he was once so proud of. On top of that, his spine was noticeably tweaked to one side, and every bone and muscle in his body ached constantly. Mentally and emotionally he was different, too, as he now knew the truth about his fractured family and how he had come to live in California.

His experiences in the polio ward had given him more understanding and compassion for troubled or injured individuals, whatever their disability, be it physical, mental, or societal. Harboring bitterness about negative events in his life wasn't a viable option for George, especially not after all the kindness he had received during his stay in the hospital. He felt especially grateful to his father, who had stood by his side throughout the long ordeal. George figured the only logical and righteous attitude to adopt was one of gratitude for just being alive and having people who cared about him, even if he had to accept that he might never see his mother again. How he was going to manifest his gratitude was the question he didn't yet have the answer to.

That night as he gazed at the star-shaped ornament that once belonged to his mother, he came up with a grand idea. Next Christmas, he would decorate their house like a Christmas wonderland. Friends and neighbors would be awestruck by the beauty of multiple Christmas trees, snowdrifts, waterfalls, winding paths, and wishing wells. It would be the best Christmas celebration anyone had ever experienced. He'd incorporate everything he had learned from his mother about Christmas: that it was a special time when people freely shared food, good cheer, and love. It was especially a time to share these gifts with others who had less. George thought about the dozens of people who had helped him through the lowest point in his life. With so many people to thank, George decided his Christmas House would have to be more beautiful and fantastic than anything they had ever seen.

Chapter 4 - First Steps

George was blinded by the intense sunlight when his father wheeled him out the front doors of the Los Angeles County General Hospital on the morning of April 22, 1936. He felt like he was being pushed into a blast furnace, and part of him wished his dad would make a quick U-turn back into the shade and security of the hospital. But when he glanced back at the nurses and fellow patients watching and waving, he knew there was no turning back, especially after all the ruckus he had made about hydrotherapy, extra massages, and the power of positive thinking. At that moment, he realized he wasn't just George Skinner, polio survivor; now he had become a role model for victims of polio and other disabilities, much as President Roosevelt was his role model. George applied the brakes on the wheelchair, startling his father. Albert assumed something was wrong with the chair and immediately set to figuring out what it was.

"I'm walking the rest of the way to the car," George said. Albert rolled his eyes but reluctantly assisted him to his feet. With steel braces on his legs, a cane in one hand, and his father propping up his

other side, George hobbled to the old Studebaker. When he was finally settled in the backseat, he looked back at the cheering crowd. George was overwhelmed and flashed a thumbs-up to the hospital workers and ambulatory patients who had gathered to watch his departure. It was the day before his birthday, and George couldn't have wished for a better gift.

On the drive home, the old neighborhood of Boyle Heights looked much worse than it had the last time he'd seen it. Cars sat idle, with fuel costs at a premium. Unkempt lawns, peeling paint, and disrepair seemed to be the norm. George knew these must be signs of unemployment and the economic depression, not laziness or slovenliness on the part of

Just out of the hospital, George wears a body brace designed to support his torso and right arm, 1936

George stands at the gym built by Albert in their backyard, 1936

George begins a regular exercise regime to regain weight and muscle mass

their neighbors. George told his father, "These people need something to cheer them up, to give them a sense of pride in the neighborhood and themselves."

There was a large group of friends and neighbors standing in front of George and Albert's house on Mathews Street when they pulled up. When George pushed the car door open, they burst into "For He's a Jolly Good Fellow." A few women wiped away tears, and others gasped as they watched George slowly emerge from the car. They were stunned by how physically impaired and withered he looked — he was not the muscular athlete they remembered. His spine was crooked and his arms were skin and bone. However, his shocking appearance didn't prevent a single person in attendance from giving George a big, sincere hug. Albert stood by the car flabbergasted. He had told a few

Homemade railings aid George as he struggles to regain muscle strength

people George would be arriving today, but he had been concerned that no one would show up for the homecoming. More than forty people had come to show their support, including Allison and her new husband.

The crowd parted when George slowly made his way toward the three front steps. Albert offered assistance, which George refused. Silence reigned as George paused at the first step to gather himself for the ascent. His knew his leg muscles weren't all there, and he wasn't positive he could make it up to the porch. He turned to the crowd and said, "I feel like I'm about to ascend Mount Everest." Everyone laughed and then quieted down as George lifted one leg and then the other, pausing after each step to catch his breath and prepare for the next. When he finally arrived at the front door, the crowd burst into cheers.

On the dining table were George's favorite foods: chicken potpie, peas, and chocolate cake for dessert, all home cooked by the ladies from the Lorena Baptist Church. Once the dinner was over and the dishes washed, the two men were left alone. George was beat from all the activity and got into his bed. Albert stowed George's belongings in his bureau and closet. He then carefully unpacked the dreaming star and hung it over the bed. "Lights-out," Albert said. "I have

A bucket loaded with gravel gives George a resistance workout to strengthen his arm muscles

Walking up and down the steps helps
strengthen George's leg muscles

to go to work tomorrow at the machine shop. Sweet dreams, Sonny," and he gave the star a spin. "'Night, Pops," said George.

George slept for an hour but woke up startled; something was wrong. It took him a minute to realize what woke him. There was no coughing, no squeaky bedsprings, and no sound of the iron lungs — it was too quiet. Unable to get back to sleep, he used the time to figure out how to transform his small bungalow into his vision of the true Christmas fairyland. There were certain traditional decorations that must be included, such as a Christmas tree, ornaments, and strings of lights. But that wasn't enough — there had to be more, lots more! Why just one Christmas tree? Why not an entire forest of Christmas trees? Why not a live Santa Claus to hand out presents and spread good cheer? And how about using real snow, not just a few wads of cotton?

George wasn't the type to dwell on the difficult aspects of his plan. Sure, the fact that he intended to create a winter wonderland in the middle of seasonless Southern California was far-fetched, but that made it all the more challenging and fun. He was mildly worried about the fact that he and his father had no savings and lived paycheck to paycheck, but he said to himself, "Where there's a will, there's a way."

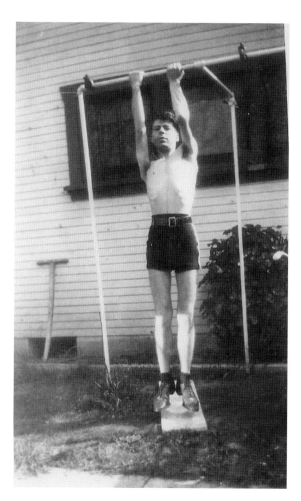

George attempts pull-ups on the outdoor gym

His mind was bombarded with dozens of ideas for bringing the house to life and the means and ways to accomplish each one. He knew he should write his inspirations down so he wouldn't forget them, so he painstakingly strapped on his leg braces and quietly inched his way to the kitchen table, careful not to wake his father. It was then that he drew the first sketches of what he would eventually call the Christmas House. He filled page after page with renderings from his imagination of how the house might look with different decorations, from different angles. He drew a waterfall and how it might flow into a meandering stream. He drew pictures of the backyard with snow-covered trees, winding pathways, and even a wishing well. As the night wore on, he made calculations of necessary supplies and the associated costs. Without a doubt, he would need donations of labor and material from friends, neighbors, and maybe local businesses. He worked until his drafting pencil was worn to a nub.

In between the drawings and calculations, he wrote autobiographical notes about the major events in his life and the feelings he had experienced. He wrote about his arrival in Los Angeles as a child, his romance with Allison, his near-drowning in the pool when the polio first struck, the hydrotherapy, his first steps, and

George spends hours on this stationary bicycle to improve his reflexes and leg muscles

the homecoming. He even wrote about his anger at his father when he had heard the letter from Lily, and about how he came to forgive his father. He wrote how that pain — and that forgiveness — was part of his recovery. The last event on the list was his vision of the Christmas House, the gift he would give to all those who had helped him. George finally laid his weary head on the table and fell asleep.

At sunrise, Albert entered the kitchen and was surprised to see George. "Son, what are you doing? You need to get to bed," he said. He pointed to the pile of papers filled with sketches and musings and asked, "What's all this about?"

"It's my plan for giving something back to everyone who's helped me," George explained. Bemused, Albert insisted that George go to bed and said they would talk about it later.

Over the next few weeks, Albert reluctantly listened to George's scheme of converting their home into the Christmas House. George pleaded for his father's assistance, physical and financial. He praised his father's mechanical abilities, his skills as a carpenter, plumber, and electrician. He proclaimed his father a master of all trades. Albert squirmed in his chair as George continued. "What better way to thank all the people who helped us out in our time of trouble?

George demonstrates his daily workout designed to strengthen weak muscles

They're still helping us, transporting me to physical therapy twice a week and bringing us food and providing moral support. It's the least we can do. This neighborhood needs something to bring everybody together, to boost their spirits. Besides, Christmas isn't what it should be. The bad economy has taken a major toll. Everyone is worried about not having enough money for gifts for their children or even for Christmas dinner."

George now had his father's undivided attention. Albert realized there was no stopping George once he started something. He was more amazed by his son's boundless energy than the grandiose idea of the Christmas House. Most people who faced a setback like polio would be too exhausted to initiate a gigantic construction project. Who was he to deprive George of something so important to him, and something very good for his morale? He mulled it over and finally said, "I'll do whatever it takes. I'll work double shifts to get the money for materials, but we'll still need a lot of help from others."

The next day George called friends, neighbors, merchants, the neighborhood American Legion Post, and even the minister of their church. His powers of persuasion and his enthusiasm made it hard for anyone to say no. By week's end, thirty volunteers, or as

George called them, "Christmas House Elves," agreed to help with the project.

George composed a letter of appreciation for those who had helped him through his ordeal with polio and who volunteered to assist with the construction of the Christmas House. Albert delivered the handwritten notes the next morning.

Thanks to you, I now know the true meaning of giving. When polio first hit me, I was literally afraid to pray because I blamed God for striking me down. The despair I felt during my hospital stay was more than I could bear alone. It was your prayers, your kindnesses, and your love that saved me. Alone, I wasn't able to overcome the ravages of polio. May the Christmas House be a small symbol of my gratitude to all of you wonderful folk. May the magic of the Christmas House touch your hearts as you have touched mine.

Signed, George G. Skinner

By Thanksgiving, the Skinner residence looked like a salvage yard with chicken wire, lumber, sacks of cement, and dead tree trunks filling the driveway, the backyard, and the garage. Albert installed pipe railings in dangerous areas of the backyard, which allowed George safe access to the various construction projects. Physically, George was making huge strides, and to improve his muscle tone, Albert rigged makeshift exercise equipment in the side yard with buckets of gravel tied to pulleys that served as free weights. Twice a day, George exercised on the homemade machine, adding extra grains of gravel as his muscle strength improved. Curious pedestrians couldn't help staring at George as he worked out on the strange-looking contraption.

Ten days before the grand opening, the Skinner house was teeming with activity. Albert cooked meals for the hungry crew after working overtime to secure the funds needed to complete the various projects. He assured George they had enough money to cover the costs. To illustrate the point, Albert cashed his weekly paycheck into one-dollar bills and spread the bills out on the living room floor. Then, George and Albert divided the bills into piles that went toward individual projects. In total, they invested over two hundred dollars on materials, an impressive sum in 1936.

Albert arrived home from work two days before the unveiling to find that all the furniture was missing from the living room. In its place stood a forest of twelve eight-foot-tall Christmas trees. He was further surprised to see that George had gutted the kitchen cabinets and with the help of some of the volunteers built the framework for new cabinets and a countertop. This particular project touched Albert deeply, as he was an accomplished cook and frequently complained about the state of the old kitchen. George calmed Albert's worries about the expense of remodeling the kitchen, explaining that he was using leftover building materials. It was just another way for George to put his pent-up energy and enthusiasm to work. His dream projects fueled him, and there was no turning back now.

With a feeling of triumph, George says good-bye to his body brace, 1936

Chapter 5 ~ Magic Time

The anticipation of George's Christmas House opening was creating quite a buzz in the neighborhood. Volunteers worked tirelessly to turn George's displays into reality. One of his ideas was to bury tree trunks upside down in holes dug in the backyard. He thought the twisted roots would resemble leafless tree branches in the dead of winter. While the workers were burying the knurly trunks, Margaret Gillingham, a neighbor and diligent volunteer, said to George, "Don't you think live Christmas trees would look a lot better?"

"Trust me, the effect will be striking," George replied. "Live trees are out of the question. They're too expensive. Look here." He pointed to the stumps in the yard. "Now, squint your eyes. Don't they look like a row of aspen trees in winter? They'll be especially beautiful at night, all lit up by floodlights."

All of a sudden, someone yelled, "timber," as one of the trunks fell over. "You have to bury it deeper, or someone is going to get hurt," George instructed. Four volunteers began digging the hole deeper. George shook another tree to test its stability. Satisfied, he painted the exposed roots and trunk with white paint. He then sprinkled metal shavings on the wet paint. Albert had brought the shavings home from the machine shop to save the cost of buying real glitter at the dime store.

The living room transformed into a holiday forest, with hand-painted mountain lane in background and "snow" covering the floor, Mathews Street, 1936

George stood back to admire his handiwork. "Not bad," he said.

The upside-down trees lined the pathway leading to a wishing well, which would prove to be one of the most popular attractions of the Christmas House.

On the sunny afternoon of the grand opening on December 15, 1936, volunteers dressed as Santa's

The original Christmas House at 919 Mathews Street, in the glaring California sun, 1936

elves were scattered about the property — two on the roof rigging lights, six in the kitchen baking, five working on the trees in the backyard, and the rest sweeping and cleaning. Many displays were still unfinished, and time was running out. "Four more hours," George hollered. "Our guests will start arriving in four short hours!" He checked on the progress of one project after another and lent a hand as needed. The fact that he hadn't slept much the past few nights made him feel as

though he was sleepwalking. He had to ask himself, "Is this really happening, or am I dreaming in my hospital bed?"

Albert was ready to test the many strands of lightbulbs and the spotlights atop the backyard castle and roof. He then called George over to witness the historic moment. But when he flipped the circuit breaker, every glass fuse on the circuit board blew from being overloaded. "Either we disconnect some lights, or this will happen every time," Albert said.

George calculated the load on his clipboard, "Let's see. Seventy-five light strands, times sixty watts, plus five floodlights and the sound system…no wonder!" He figured they were drawing twice the electricity allotted by the power company. Not to be undone, George immediately telephoned the Los Angeles

Department of Water and Power and spoke to the superintendent. When George told him the *Herald Express* was sending a reporter to cover the opening of the Christmas House, the manager gladly offered to loan him an emergency generator. George assured the superintendent that he would mention the generous donation to the reporter.

On the roof, next to the façade of a redbrick chimney, was a realistic Santa Claus fashioned from plywood and painted by Albert. Over Santa's shoulder was a huge gunnysack spilling over with fake presents. The roof appeared to be covered in two feet of snow, which was actually cornflakes mixed with white cotton batting.

The sun was getting low in the sky, and the holiday festivities were scheduled to begin at dusk. George went into the kitchen to join the bucket brigade, who were passing large chunks of ice from the icebox to a chipping station on the front porch. Elves scattered the chipped ice on the front lawn and steps, giving the Los Angeles lawn the look of freshly fallen snow. They then scattered mica chips on the ice to give it a sparkly look. The brigade repeated this process all evening long since the temperature was in the seventies and the ice melted quickly.

Most houses in the neighborhood had a simple

The Christmas House lit up for its debut, 1936

wreath on the front door or a decorated Christmas tree visible though the front window. The Skinner house was another story, something no one had ever seen before. Sure, a few department stores downtown had window displays and hired men to dress as Santa Claus, but nothing compared to this extravaganza.

The energy level was extremely high at the Christmas House, as at the opening night of a Broadway show. As night fell, Albert started up the borrowed generator, triggering the illumination of row after row of lights.

The audio system was George's passion. He had converted an old phonograph and some scavenged tube amplifiers into a one-man recording and broadcasting studio. His Rube Goldberg contraption enabled him to cut his own 78 rpm records. The previous Sunday, he had recorded members of the church choir singing Christmas carols. He intended to broadcast their voices throughout the neighborhood with speakers strategically hidden in man-made snowdrifts facing the street.

"Is everybody ready for Christmas?" George hollered,

Boyle Heights neighbors wait in line for the opening of the Christmas House, 1936

memories of his time in the iron lung all but forgotten. A chorus of "Ready!" rang out. He set the phonograph needle on the record and turned the volume up to as high as it would go. "Oh come all ye faithful, joyful and triumphant..." The carol could be heard a block away, and strangers followed the sound to the small bungalow on Mathews Street. A young couple with two children happened to be taking an evening stroll past the Skinner residence when George cranked up the holiday music. The father was startled and reached protectively for his children. The little girl saw Santa Claus on the roof and pointed, saying, "Look, Dad, it's Santa Claus." Her father realized his mistake and released his excited children. The little boy made a snowball out of the shaved ice on the lawn and threw it at his father, who reciprocated, all in good fun. Albert emerged from the house dressed as one of Santa's elves and

JURY MAY GIVE WERNER CASE VERDICT TODAY

Panel Will Be Allowed to Deliberate Until 10 P. M.; 'Black Book' Rejected as Evidence

Tonight may bring a verdict in the month-long Werner-Weinblatt liquor permit trial, but its political repercussions may resound indefinitely in local and state political circles.

Arguments are to be completed before the end of the day. Superior Judge Charles W. Fricke will give the jury its instructions in less than an hour, and it virtually had been decided yesterday to let the six men and six women deliberate until 10 p. m.

If unable to reach a verdict by that hour, they would be taken to their quarters in the Rosslyn Hotel to resume the debate at 9 a. m. tomorrow.

Chief item of the possible aftermath of the sensational politico-criminal trial of Helen Werner, her husband, Erwin "Pete" Werner, and Joseph Weinblatt, is Mrs. Werner's "black book," an office memorandum which Deputy District Attorneys Eugene Williams and George Stahlman were unable to place in evidence because of the cryptic nature of its jottings, but which they now propose to refer to the county grand jury.

TO QUIZ MANY

That body, searching for the meaning of the notes, would be expected by the district attorney's office to summon a large number of local and state political notables whose names occur and recur in the little diary.

The book disappeared from Mrs. Werner's office during last

"Believe It or Not"

SNOWSTORM IN LOS ANGELES

GEORGE SKINNER—AND HE'S SWEEPING SNOW
It's Falling as He Sweeps—Big Flakes, Too—But It's Artificial
—International News Photo by Los Angeles Examiner.

WALKER RITES SLATED TODAY

Maybe it doesn't snow in Los Angeles. Maybe the cameraman was seeing things. Maybe the camera was, too.

But there, sure as life, was George Skinner, of 919 South Mathews street, sweeping the snow off his front walk. It fell even as he swept. It covered his

dulging in the vigorous winter sports.

His hobby is decorating his home for Christmas. And judging from the "ahs" and "ohs" from the children of the nearby Soto Street School, his artificial snow this year might be real as well as not the

WOMAN'S BODY FOUND IN SURF

Plaything of the surf, the body of Rose Finkelstein, winter visitor from Chicago, was found off the foot of Navy street in Venice yesterday afternoon.

Efforts were being made to contact relatives in Chicago last night.

Miss Finkelstein was said to have come here for the winter in an effort to recuperate from a nervous breakdown.

Authorities were undecided whether she fell accidentally from a pier or committed suicide.

On Sundays the Examiner can do your sales job alone. Make its display columns your first selling ally.

HAL EX TO ALTER

James F. Fall, N ist, who recently guilty to a charge tortion letters to actress, today is change his plea be Judge Albert Lee.

The youthful confession, accord ment of Justice torney, Ames Peters yesterday that h decided that it wou of time" to deman

Miss Rogers wa and her mother, w ers, would be kill left $50000 at a Lo for the writer of notes.

Clipping from the Los Angeles Examiner showing George sweeping "snow," December 21, 1936

welcomed visitors inside, acting as their tour guide. He walked them through the indoor forest of trees and led them into the kitchen, where he served them Christmas cookies and apple cider.

Meanwhile, George changed into his costume in the bedroom. His outfit looked like a cross between a jester's and an elf's, but at least it was red and green, and the price was right — free. He couldn't believe that the moment he had long dreamed of was finally here. He gazed at the star over his bed and spoke. "You know, this Christmas House is for you, Mother. We'll show these people what a real Christmas is. Merry Christmas, Mom, wherever you are." George looked out the front window and watched his father graciously welcoming more guests. He knew his decision to forgive his dad for past mistakes had been the right thing to do. The alternative, to hold a grudge, was not a character trait he wanted.

By the time George was on the front porch, the line of people waiting to visit the Christmas House stretched halfway down the block. Everyone was in a festive mood as they waited in line. George recognized neighbors who were unemployed and suffering, and even they were in good spirits.

The Christmas House was doing exactly what it was supposed to do: inspire people to set aside their problems and share in the joy of the season. The whole neighborhood felt different. It was invigorated and tightly knit, like one big family. Neighbors of every nationality and race, even some with long-standing feuds, were enjoying one another's company. For the next three weeks, through Christmas Day, thousands of visitors from outside Boyle Heights toured the house and had a ball, especially the children.

One of George's cleverest ideas was to place a microphone and speaker inside the wishing well in the backyard. They enabled him to hear and mysteriously answer the wishes of guests while he hid in the garage. The talking wishing well became a favorite with children who wanted a particular Christmas gift. He was deeply touched by the children's sincerity as they expressed their wishes and dreams. Sometimes the children's requests were so hysterically funny he had to cover the microphone until his laughing fit subsided. Other times, he gently convinced the children that a more practical and less extravagant gift might be a better choice; he knew most of the parents in the neighborhood had very little to spend on Christmas.

On December 20, a reporter from the *Los Angeles Times* arrived and approached Albert. He wanted to know where the idea for the Christmas House had come from. Albert told the reporter George had concocted it while laid up in the hospital with polio. George agreed to have his picture taken in front of the house, but being the consummate showman, he first wanted to set the stage. He returned with a bucket of white cornflakes and a house fan. Two of his favorite elves, Margaret Gillingham and Audrey Dunken, joined him, while another elf dumped the flakes into the blades of the spinning fan, creating the illusion of a blinding snowstorm. George and his lady elves stood in the middle of the blizzard, and the reporter took their picture.

When the *Times* arrived on the Skinner doorstep the next morning, Albert nearly tripped as he unfolded it. On the front page was the picture of George, Audrey, and Margaret in the snow. The caption explained that the photograph wasn't taken in Alaska or Canada but sunny California. Albert was extremely proud and called, "George, George! You did it. You're on the front page of the paper." Albert immediately went to the market to buy more copies.

By Christmas Eve, the police closed the street to vehicular traffic, and the masses jammed Mathews Street. This was definitely the place to be in Los Angeles County during the holiday season of 1936.

Margaret Gillingham, Audrey Dunken, and George featured on the front page of the *Los Angeles Times*, December 21, 1936

Chapter 6 ~ In the Heart of Wonderland

The Los Angeles Police estimated that over 80,000 visitors made the pilgrimage to the Skinner house during its second season in 1937. George and Albert had incorporated every Christmas fantasy a child or adult could imagine, and then some. No one could resist the delight of seeing the modest bungalow decorated with regal and whimsical Christmas embellishments. Even politicians and movie stars flocked to the homemade fairyland. Rumor had it that someone spotted Walt Disney among the throngs that year.

George's health had vastly improved. He was developing good muscle tone and increased lung capacity from all the physical activity involved in the construction of his wonderland. The only giveaways that he was a polio survivor were his limp and his ever-present cane. With his cheerful grin and his strikingly handsome features, he was frequently mistaken for a movie star. For all intents and purposes, the Christmas House was a movie set, and he was the writer, the director, and indeed, the star.

Christmas House "elves" from the American Legion Post join Albert and George, donning uniforms made by the ladies

George painting the roof of the cottage in the backyard, 1937

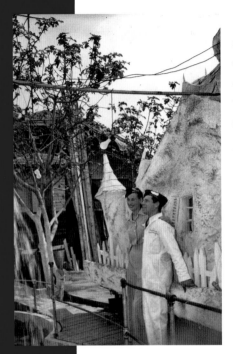

Posing for photographers, George and a volunteer admire the backyard fairyland

George's boundless energy and optimism magnetized men and women alike. Women often approached him to volunteer their labor, when actually they coveted his companionship. He adroitly sublimated their passion for him into a passion for the Christmas House. Soon they were eager and productive elves. In the name of publicity, George allowed a reporter to photograph a group of female elves playing in the snow on the front lawn clad only in bathing suits. This time, the snow was real, sent by refrigerated rail car from Utah.

With so many willing and able helpers, George turned his attention to completing the remodel of the kitchen. Many of the neighborhood workers contributed time and leftover building materials to help the Skinners create a state-of-the-art kitchen. In addition, George enlisted the help of one of Albert's relatives, Dorothy Fee, who worked at the new Sears store that had recently opened in Los Angeles. She arranged a payment plan for George and Albert so that they could afford the appliances and electric gadgets in the latest streamlined designs. They had little money to invest in their modern kitchen, but

"Elves" from the American Legion Post explore the display

their ingenuity and persuasiveness helped them complete it.

The kitchen was an accomplishment George was very proud of. Wearing a pin-striped suit and an apron, he demonstrated the appliances while his friend, the well-known local photographer Dick Whittington, took photographs. The story and pictures appeared in the Southern California Gas Company *Gas News*, which had over 20,000 readers. In the near future, George hoped to include the pictures in a portfolio that would land him a job as a designer at a film studio. He and Albert used the kitchen to prepare elaborate meals at monthly dinner parties, spending very little money but impressing their guests. Frequently in attendance were Preston Goddard and his wife. Preston had been one of the therapists assigned to work with George during his stay in the polio ward and had eventually been in charge of all of George's treatments. He marveled at the work George had now accomplished.

~

George and Albert wasted little time resting on the laurels of the success of the second year of the Christmas House. By springtime of 1938, they were busy completing projects that included a footbridge over a man-made creek and a twenty-foot-tall castle in the backyard.

The Skinners' newly modernized kitchen showed off George's interior design skills

Article about the Skinners' modern kitchen in the Gas News, 1937

The news media hounded George and Albert, wanting to know every detail of the new and improved Christmas House. George made it easy for the reporters; he wrote a press release himself and handed out copies at a special gathering the night before the public opening. The press release read:

Four years after polio struck, George balances atop a crooked picket fence while Albert adds the final touches to the backyard snow mountain, 1938

George builds his winter dreamland with used chicken wire and plaster

This Christmas, amidst a neighborhood of modest homes in the Boyle Heights District of Los Angeles, will stand the most unique house in the world. It is the creation of Albert and George Skinner, a father and son team who have taken the art of decorating one's home at the holidays to a new level. Last year, they attracted thousands with their re-creation of Christmas symbols from around the world, but this year they plan to outdo themselves. New additions this year will include eight life-size reindeer on the roof towing a sleigh with Santa Claus aboard. The roof will be covered in snow, as well as the front and back yards. Santa's elves will graciously serve visitors homemade pastries with hot apple cider and whole milk. In the backyard, a waterfall will cascade from an ice glacier. The children will delight in romping around a replica of Snow White's cottage and wishing well in the backyard.

It seemed that every few weeks another article or photograph would appear in the local newspapers, announcing that the Christmas House would be open from December 10 to January 10. And George's vision had extended far beyond Los Angeles, as newspapers from all over the country picked up the story.

George's writing skills were well honed after his studies in business during college, and he used these skills not only to promote the Christmas House but also to secure donations from food distributors, Hollywood studios, and other businesses. Movie studios donated or loaned props and costumes. The local power company donated electricity, an emergency generator, and expertise. Wholesale food distributors gladly supplied plenty of food and drink for visitors. George used his charm and persuasiveness to secure these donations.

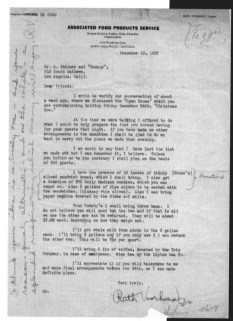

Letter outlines the company's generous donation of food

Collage of Eastside Journal article from December 16, 1937, flanked by photographs of the Christmas House

His phone calls, letters, and personal visits left little room for "no." Ruth Voorhees of Associated Food Products wrote back, "The reason I am happy to do this is because I think your idea is a lovely one and your reason purely altruistic. On the whole — a splendid inspiration, which many will enjoy."

In October of 1938, George and Albert were obliged to move into the garage to make room for the forest of Christmas trees located in nearly every room of the house. Albert insisted the newly remodeled kitchen be left operational because it was essential for the preparation of Christmas delicacies.

Unbeknownst to Albert, George built a three-foot replica of the wishing star that had belonged to his mother. He mounted it atop the water tower in the backyard and wired it with lights. George thought of the star as a tribute to his mother. When Albert saw the star lit up one night on his way home from work, he knew exactly what it symbolized. No words were necessary between father and son. The true meaning of the star was their secret. To visitors it was just another beautiful decoration, representing a bright star in the December sky.

Prior to opening day, December 10, 1938, every newspaper in the Los Angeles area carried headlines about the Christmas House, such as "Snow to Order"

and "White Christmas Right Here in Town." Radio shows nationwide frequently discussed the house as well. Letters came in from across the country, praising George and Albert's accomplishment and optimistic message.

Fir trees create a small forest beneath the dream castle in the clouds against a wall of tin in the Skinner backyard

Among the crowds waiting in line for a preview of the Christmas House on December 8, two days before the grand opening in 1938, was Pearl Majoros, the nurse's aide who had transcribed George's letter to President and Mrs. Roosevelt. She waved and shouted

The front page of the Los Angeles Examiner features the Christmas House, December 10, 1937

from amongst the throngs on the sidewalk. Finally, she managed to catch George's attention, but he didn't recognize her. He politely waved back, but she was just another pretty face in the crowd. Pearl was disheartened since she felt she had a special connection with George. She knew how far he'd come. Unable to work her way through the crowd to talk to him, she left a note in the mailbox congratulating him on his recovery and accomplishments. Her phone number was scribbled on the note, but she had little hope he would call her.

Later that evening, while George was giving a tour of the backyard to a group of newspaper reporters, he noticed the crowd noise growing louder. He looked back at the house and saw black smoke billowing from the roof. Albert ran out the back door yelling for buckets of water. But it was too late — and too dangerous — to enter the house and combat the fire. The living room was fully engulfed, and the windows burst out from the heat. Guests stood in the middle of the street watching the flames consume the little house. George bravely attempted to enter the house in order to save mementos, but the smoke overcame him. He was assisted back to the safety of the street, barely able to breathe.

It seemed like forever before the fire trucks arrived. After the firefighters doused the flames, it was obvious that the house was nearly destroyed. The Christmas House was gone. More in shock than seriously injured, George agreed to be taken by ambulance to the hospital for observation. As the ambulance pulled away, George couldn't believe he was on his way to the same hospital where he had been treated for polio. "Please God," he thought, "don't keep me away for long this time." He looked back at the house just as the lights on the wishing star twinkled on and off, on and off, and then stayed on. George figured the emergency generator must have kicked in. "No," he said to himself, "I won't be gone long this time."

Chapter 7 ~ Snowflakes and Ashes

The inferno started in the living room, and the source of combustion was a smoldering cigarette. Based on eyewitness testimony, a fire inspector determined that a couple had slipped under the ropes before the official preview opened. They proceeded to gallivant about, exploring the house and playing hide-and-seek behind the trees and decorations. Evidently, the man dropped a lit cigarette in the living room, and the sap of a Christmas tree acted as an accelerant. Within minutes the Skinners' living room was a raging forest fire that nearly destroyed everything they owned.

The next day reporters were on the scene, taking photographs of the destruction and quizzing Albert about plans for the future. He evaded answering all questions until his son was released from the hospital with a clean bill of health later that afternoon. The doctors said there was nothing they could do for George's broken heart, however. He couldn't stop thinking about the planning, the labor, and the donations that went for naught. He wasn't sad for himself or his father but for the children who loved visiting

The day after the fire, inspectors review the damage, December 9, 1938

the Christmas House. The previous year, thousands of children had waited in line to talk to Santa Claus, to see and play with snow for the first time in their lives, and to ask the talking wishing well for their hearts' desires — in short, to experience the wonder of Christmas.

Albert surveys the extensive damage to the living room

When Albert informed his son that their home-owner's insurance policy had lapsed before the fire, George was beside himself. Albert explained that every paycheck had gone toward supplies for the Christmas House, and when the insurance bill came, he simply didn't have enough money left to pay the premium. The fire department estimated the damage at more than $10,000.

For the next few days father and son sifted through the rubble, all the while discussing whether to rebuild or hire a bulldozer. The fire had ravaged most of the interior of the house; only their two small bed-rooms were spared, although both rooms suffered severe smoke and water damage. The new kitchen was completely destroyed and would have to be gutted and rebuilt from scratch. They decided to make the best of the situation and moved into the garage, which was still intact.

Their neighbors in Boyle Heights rallied to help George and Albert with basic necessities, and some even invited them to sleep in their homes until their house was again habitable. George and Albert respect-fully turned down the kind offers and joked about how much they enjoyed living in the garage. George said, "Living in the garage is a minor inconvenience. It's nothing compared to what I went through with polio."

George noticed that most children who walked by the house looked as if they were passing by a funeral, as if Christmas was gone forever. Not comprehending the

YULE HOUSE SAVED . . . BUT HIS HOME BURNS

For two years, George G. Skinner, former paralytic, has made a hobby of his Christmas House—enlarging it, painting, decorating. Last year the fairyland exhibit drew 85,000 visitors. Yesterday, a seven-minute burst of flame destroyed Skinner's own home, a few feet away. The Christmas scene in his backyard, however, was unscarred, and may be opened tomorrow. Above, left, Skinner is shown at work on the exhibit. At right, he surveys damage to his own home. (Story on Page I-II.)

—Los Angeles Examiner photos.

Los Angeles Examiner article announces the reopening within days of the fire

extent of the damage, one young girl stopped to stare at the pile of ashes and asked George how soon the Christmas House would reopen. He replied that he wasn't sure. He couldn't bring himself to say "next year" or "never." That would have been such a letdown for her. Instead, he said, "We'll still open. Don't worry."

George couldn't stop thinking how disappointed all the children would be if the Christmas House didn't open this year. He approached his father and said, "So what if no one can go inside the house? The backyard decorations are intact. If we don't have some kind of Christmas celebration, the children will be devastated. After New Year's, we can focus on rebuilding the house. For now, the whole neighborhood — in fact, all of Los Angeles — is counting on us to provide the children with a place to celebrate the Christmas spirit."

George shovels "snow" on the front lawn as spectators wait to enter the reopened Christmas House

An unidentified visitor gazes into the magic cottage

Albert knew it didn't matter what he said. Sound logic never was king in the Skinner household anyway. The Christmas House was going to open this year no matter what he thought, and they shook hands on it.

Word soon spread that George and Albert were reopening the Christmas House despite the damage, and more volunteers than ever showed up with shovels, rakes, and wheelbarrows. Men, women, and children from as far away as San Diego shoveled and swept debris from the property, and then they trucked it away. All the items that could be salvaged, such as fragments of photographs, furniture, and decorations, were stacked in the garage for George and Albert to sort through later.

George looked for the wishing star in his bedroom. The metal hook over his bed that the ornament had once hung from was still there, but the treasured star was nowhere to be found. He guessed it may have melted from the heat or been blasted away by the water hoses. George told everyone, "Be on the lookout for a small tin star. It looks like the one on the water tower. It is more important to me than anything else."

Nothing in the living room was salvageable; the intense heat had burned everything beyond recognition. Even the metal doorbell chime was a melted glob on the living room floor. The pressure of the firemen's water hoses had blown charred bits of furniture, carpeting, and decorations into waterlogged piles.

Albert's bedroom suffered the least damage since it was at the rear of the house. While searching for clean clothes that might fit him, George noticed an old metal box in Albert's closet. Curious, he pulled it

out and opened it. Inside he found a stack of letters, all with the return address of Lily Palmer, Hamilton, Ontario, Canada. His heart skipped a beat, as all the

Albert and George look over bills in front of their charred home where a sign announces the revised opening date

pent-up feelings of longing for his mother and brothers hit him at once. He hesitantly opened the top letter, dated June 1938.

"Dearest Albert, I have just been informed of the

whereabouts of your sons…" The letter went on to ask him to please let her know if she should make contact with them. Underneath the letter was a newspaper clipping with a photo of a group of high school graduates. George carefully scanned the picture and, sure enough, he saw a young man who closely resembled what he thought his brother Gordon might look like.

George didn't take the time to read the rest of the letters. He had seen enough. He found it unbelievable that his father had hidden the letters from him after all they had been through. Lily was his aunt, not just his father's sister. And his brothers were his brothers, not just his father's sons. He had a right to hear any and all news about them, and his father had promised him that when he was in the hospital. George's shock turned to outrage. Feeling betrayed, he stormed into the kitchen, waved

George puts the finishing touches on the backyard display that dwarfs the house in the background

the letter in his father's face, and demanded an explanation.

Albert feebly tried to convince him that contact with Gordon and Walter might have devastating consequences. "Your brothers have a good life in Canada. Corresponding with them now may do more harm than good. It's been so long; I have to approach this in the right way at the right time. If I were in a position to offer them a home here in Los Angeles, I would do it in an instant. But the fire dashed any hope of that happening. I promise you we'll get in touch with your brothers, but not now, not with our lives in a state of turmoil."

Once again George forgave his father, saying, "My heart breaks whenever I think of them." He knew his father's intentions were noble, so why did his actions so often break people's hearts? George wouldn't blame his brothers if they never forgave their father. But for him it would be senseless to resent his father; right now, they needed each other more than ever. Yet George felt abandoned by his father and his mother. Vowing to never treat others this way, he put his energy into the one thing that could brighten his spirits — rebuilding the Christmas House.

At the same time, George secretly began devising his own plan to contact his lost family. Without informing Albert, he wrote a press release about the Christmas House. He emphasized the names George, Albert, and Skinner as many times as grammatically possible. He hand-delivered it to the United Press Wire Service in downtown Los Angeles and asked them to specifically target Canadian newspapers and radio stations. With any luck, his brothers or his mother would read the article, recognize the names, and contact them.

The next day the headlines of the *Los Angeles Herald Express* read "Fire Fails to Halt Spirit of Yuletide." The article quoted George as saying, "You can tell the children of Los Angeles that the fire won't rob them of the opportunity to experience Christmas at the Skinner house. It will be better than ever, with waterfalls and live trout in the winding waterways. We will be open for visitors by the twentieth of December."

Miraculously, the burnt-out bungalow was reopened as the Christmas House on December 19. The

Los Angeles Evening News reports on the fire that destroyed the Christmas House, December 9, 1938

damage from the fire was disguised with carefully placed cotton batting and tree branches that hid the tarps covering debris. Albert had painted a new plywood Santa Claus that stood near the front door, and the whimsical white picket fence still bordered the lawn. The tower in the backyard with its tin star on top was lit every night. Over one hundred and fifty singers from various church choirs around Los Angeles donated their time and beautiful voices every evening, and Christmas carols filled the air.

THE CHRISTMAS HOUSE—Copyright by George Skinner, 1938

Postcard of the best display ever, with turned-up trees, snow mountain, cascading waterfall, cottage, and tower supporting the tin star

In spite of the fire, the newspapers reported that over 100,000 visitors toured the Christmas House that year. As far as they could discern, the magic remained, and there was no visible fire damage. The Christmas House was in perfect form, better than ever before. A few visitors did comment about the aroma of burnt wood, but they surmised that the scent was an element of staging, like chestnuts roasting on an open fire. George grew hoarse that season from disguising his voice, speaking in the gruff voice of an old wizard to many of the children making wishes at the magic wishing well.

Lest anyone forget the original Christmas House, Dick Whittington, the photographer and friend of George's, turned some of his best images of the house into postcards. Albert and George sold the postcards for two cents each, with the proceeds going toward a fund to rehabilitate their house. Fourteen-year-old Bobby Baker, visiting with his father from the Wilshire Boulevard district, bought twelve postcards with the hope that it would help with the reconstruction. He made his father promise, in front of George and Albert, that they would decorate their own house better next Christmas.

The efforts to get the Christmas House open so quickly after the fire and the lack of proper living quarters took a heavy toll on father and son. They decided this would be the last year of the Skinner Christmas House. It was someone else's turn to carry on the tradition of providing children and adults with a Christmas experience like no other. Albert pointed out that more and more families were stringing lights on their houses. He even saw one house with a life-size manger scene on the front lawn. The Skinners felt as though they had passed the torch to countless families in the area.

One well-heeled gentleman made a point of locating George during the final days of the Christmas House. He wanted to know more about the homemade recording and broadcasting studio. After a lengthy demonstration on how the scavenged and jerry-built equipment functioned, the man praised George's electro-mechanical skills and flare for the dramatic. He introduced himself as Edward Bennett, founder of a radio academy in Hollywood. He offered George a full scholarship at his radio school and told him that if he successfully passed his classes, a job would very likely be in the cards. George took the offer as divine intervention — and just in the nick of time, as the Skinners were beyond broke. He told his father, "Radio broadcasting requires all the skills I possess in the recording and mechanical arts. Hey, and those paychecks will buy lots of lumber and materials to rebuild the house."

When the last group of Christmas House visitors left on January 17, 1939, the Skinners' Christmas House on Mathews Street closed for good. George and Albert had resigned themselves to the fact that the Christmas House must be put on hold indefinitely. It was time to move on, to fulfill new dreams, and to let others carry on the tradition of celebrating Christmas with the Skinner flair.

Letter granting an extension of auxiliary power through January 15, 1939

Chapter 8 ~ Preserve Your Memories

Once the Christmas House was closed, George and Albert needed to focus on the basic elements of survival: food, shelter, and making a living. Their accommodations were only one step above camping out. Eternal optimists, they took their dilemma in stride. They frequently joked about the situation and acted like Laurel and Hardy in a movie about two guys down on their luck. Fortunately, the comedy was playing out in sunny Los Angeles where outdoor living was possible even in the middle of winter.

Because of the fire, the property was now one of the most run-down in the neighborhood. If George and Albert didn't concentrate their energies, the City of Los Angeles Department of Building and Safety might condemn their home on Mathews Street, deeming it uninhabitable for health and safety reasons. The burned-out shell of a house needed an infusion of money, and lots of it.

Offers of assistance came from adoring neighbors and church members. Out of the blue, a neighbor would appear with a hot meal, or a group of men from the church would show up with a truck to haul debris

George and Albert eating lunch in the burned-out kitchen with umbrellas ready to block the rain, 1939

to the city dump. One neighbor contributed a camp stove for cooking and heat until the natural-gas line was reconnected and a secondhand stove was found and installed. The garage now served as the living room, dining room, and kitchen. In the evenings, neighbors frequently gathered around the Skinner campfire in the backyard to reminisce and share meals. During the occasional rains, umbrellas were strategically placed so the cloudburst didn't disrupt their dining pleasure.

Albert wasn't the type to wallow in self-pity and lament their predicament. He worked ten hours a day, six days a week as a tool and die maker to provide the bare necessities. But there was no way his income alone was enough to purchase the materials or labor necessary to rehabilitate the house. George enrolled in classes at the Edward Bennett School of Radio and excelled. Mr. Bennett allowed George to work side by side with him in the studio, and this experience helped George hone his skills even more. He was excited about a career in radio broadcasting. He envisioned buying building materials, furniture, and kitchen appliances and eventually building his own recording studio with the income.

After just a month of classes and study, George became an apprentice engineer. And true to his word,

George (far right) as the lead announcer in a radio play at the Edward Bennett School of Radio, 1939

Edward Bennett offered him a job at the studio. When George received his first paycheck, he asked his father to help organize a party in honor of the volunteers who had helped build the Christmas House. He wanted to invite church members, neighbors, friends, and fellow polio survivors. Albert was in favor of the party but cautioned George about the expense. They didn't have enough money between them to cover the full cost of the party. Not to be deterred, George called the church and they agreed to ask volunteers to bring covered dishes to contribute to a festive meal. Kids in the neighborhood hand-delivered the forty-five invitations to save on postage. On the envelopes, rather than addressing the invitees formally as "Mr." or "Mrs.," George opted to use the title "Elf," as in "Elf Judd" or "Elf Goddard."

The garage that had served so well as living quarters was the site for the festivities. Even though the holiday season was long over, George and Albert decorated the garage and backyard in full Christmas regalia, and the guests were encouraged to dress in holiday attire. Christmas carols wafted from a charred but still functional gramophone. The guests shared stories about the construction of the Christmas House, and they marveled over the ingenious solutions they had devised to solve vexing problems.

When the meal was finished and the party was

George stands in front of the house while Albert pokes his head through the damaged rafters, 1939

Damaged roof in foreground and tower and displays in the background, January 1939

Some day (when we find adequate words) we are going to tell you a story of the most remarkable boy who ever entered Sawyer's. A boy who four years ago was a hopeless paralytic and has since done a great deal toward putting Los Angeles on the map, and who was mentioned by President Roosevelt in a radio address.

George Skinner's amazing achievements are little short of inspirational and seem to be, thus far, just a beginning.

Some day, George! When we find words!

Sawyer Business School newsletter column honoring George Skinner, 1939

we want to turn it around and say thanks to you. This is for you, for all you have done for us."

George wanted to savor the moment, so he unwrapped the gift very slowly. He shook it, listened to it, and sniffed it. The watching guests laughed at his antics. Inside the box was a large wooden scrapbook with the words "Christmas House Scrapbook" expertly carved into the polished, handmade cover.

Cover of the wooden scrapbook created by Preston Goddard and presented to George

winding down, Preston Goddard, the man who had directed George's treatments in the hospital, stood in the middle of the driveway and called above the noise, requesting everyone's attention. In his arms, Mr. Goddard held a beautifully wrapped present for George, a large package he had hidden outside until this moment. "George," he said. "We know you brought us all together this evening to say thanks, but

George was extremely moved by the gift and at a loss for words. Mr. Goddard took the book from George, turned to the first page, and read the inscription:

Dear George,

We wish there were words to express the happiness it has given us to see your dream come true. No words can summon up our feeling of gratitude for allowing us to partake in your wonderful fantasies. As a token of our appreciation, please accept this book of memories of the Christmas House. It made the world a better place in which to live. It lifted the spirits of thousands of children and adults. We know its legacy will continue for years to come.

Gratefully,

Mr. and Mrs. R. Preston Goddard and the Christmas House gang

Newspaper clippings had been saved and were cleverly displayed in the scrapbook

THURSDAY, DECEMBER 29, 1938   DAILY NEWS, LOS ANGELES, CALIF.

L. A. Civic Center Program

Loss of Funds Blamed on Shaw Officials

Los Angeles' proposed $26,-000,000 civic center building program has fallen through, it was announced yesterday by Mayor Fletcher Bowron, who blamed the previous administration for its failure.

The mayor made the announcement following a conference in his office with Col. Donald Connolly, Southern California works progress administration head, and Kenneth E. Godwin, regional director of the public works administration, whose offices are in San Francisco.

The mayor pinned the failure to obtain federal aid to finance the program directly on the administration of former Mayor Frank L. Shaw, whom he defeated in the September 16 recall election, and said: "The public has been kidded too long."

"The past administration," he explained, "kidded the public into believing the city was going to receive a beautiful civic center," and charged that there was a great deal of confusion and delay somewhere along the line by the old administration.

Eastside Beauty Spot Attracts

"THE CHRISTMAS HOUSE" at 919 South Mathews street, Hollenbeck Heights, has attracted 64,000 persons this season by its brilliant lighting and wintry aspect achieved by artificial snow and ice. The exhibit was conceived and created by George G. Skinner. It is shown free of charge each night. Skinner said the spectacle will remain open by popular request through January 15.—Daily News photo.

'Christmas House' On Display Until January 15

Popularity of "The Christmas House," 919 South Mathews street, Hollenbeck Heights, prompted the originator and owner George G. Skinner, to announce yesterday the colorful spectacle will remain open to the public through January 15.

Including the 18,000 persons who visited the house last Tuesday night, the total number of visitors this season has reached 64,000.

Skinner opened the house for the first time last year and was forced to delay this season's opening when fire almost destroying it last December 9. Repairs were rushed, however, and the exhibit opened three days later.

The spectacle, a veritable fairyland of unique building types, is enhanced with a covering of artificial snow and brilliant lighting effects.

Skinner is presenting "The Christmas House" free of charge under sponsorship of American Legion Sunrise post, No. 357.

The exhibit is open nightly from 6 p. m. to midnight on week days, and from 1 p. m. to midnight on weekends.

Fire Fails to Halt Spirit of Yule

Christmas House Opens Despite Difficulties

Open at last after much disappointment, including a fire that destroyed a home and "snow that marred the decorations, Los Angeles' famous Christmas House at 919 South Mathews street is shown above. Playing in the "snow" in front of the house are Joan Portland, left, and Windy Gilmore. Started several years ago by George C. Skinner in his backyard, the house attracts thousands.

Snow Falls in L. A. But It's Yule Stunt

LOS ANGELES EVENING HERALD AND EXPRESS: DECEMBER 16, 1938

Emma J. Butler Is Laid to Rest

More than thirty pages of newspaper clippings, photographs, letters, and cards were preserved in the Christmas House scrapbook

Cheers and applause rang out as George turned the pages of the scrapbook. Tears rolled down his cheeks as he viewed the photographs, cards, and letters. The book detailed George's struggles with polio and the numerous transformations of the Christmas House. It included stories from many of the characters involved. The crowd encircled George and stood rapt as he slowly turned each page.

When George regained his composure, he said, "What a long journey this has been. This gift, this memento of the Christmas House, is not for my father or for me. It is for all of us. What we did together made it important. It was a group effort, and thanks to all of you. Thank you for believing in my dream." George offered a toast: "To everyone here, and to those who couldn't be here, thank you, thank you very much. I shall cherish this gift forever."

After jubilant applause, everyone gathered around the scrapbook to view and talk about each photograph, letter, and newspaper clipping. There were plenty of pictures of each person at the party, and every turn of a page brought an exclamation like, "I can't believe it!," "Is that me?," or "Do you remember that?" Many of the photographs had been recovered from the debris of the fire and were crispy around the edges, giving the book a homey, campfire smell.

Newspaper clipping in the scrapbook features Christmas House "elves" Wendy Gilmore (left) and Jean Portland taking a "snow" shower

Santa to See Greatest Outdoor Illumination in City's History

Tree Lights Glow On Thousands of Southland Lawns

Suburbs Join In Pageant of Beauty

Los Angeles and its suburbs are all lighted up like a Christmas tree these nights.

In the yards of civic-conscious residents, in parks, in public observances, evergreen trees are bursting nightly into vari-colored splendor, constituting the greatest organized outdoor Christmas spectacle in the region's history.

General head of the movement is the women's auxiliary of the Los Angeles Chamber of Commerce, whose officers reported yesterday that the annual illumination has succeeded beyond expectations.

Notable among the decorated communities are Beverly Hills, Laurel Canyon, Highland Park, Brentwood and the Exposition Park section.

Mrs. Arthur L. Shelhorn, beautification chairman of the auxiliary, announced that a Highland Park tree lighting ceremony would be held this evening at 112 South Avenue 66, home of Dr. Louise May Richter, and that tomorrow night a public Christmas tree will be illuminated in the Cheviot Hills section at Forrester and Motor avenues.

SNOW IN Southern California? Here's a snowman sitting on a snow-covered lawn at 724 North Camden drive, waiting for Santa's arrival. This outdoor lighting scene is attracting widespread attention among sightseers. The striking effect is achieved by the use of asbestos. —*Los Angeles Examiner photo*

Christmas House Closed This Year

Because of the impossibility of satisfactory rebuilding, after damage by fire, the famous Christmas House, at 919 South Mathews street, will not be open this holiday season.

George G. Skinner, who, with his father, has annually prepared a display that has attracted thousands of visitors, said that plans are being made to move the Christmas House to a new location and rebuild it for Christmas, 1940.

By 1939, The Los Angeles Examiner reported a new trend in holiday decorations and notes the Christmas House closure

Preston Goddard asked George how he had conceived of the idea for the Christmas House in the first place. George thought about it for a minute and said, "Four and a half years ago, while I was a polio victim in the hospital and you were helping me regain strength in my arms and legs, I cheered myself up by pretending I was somewhere other than where I was. Often I imagined I was at my mother's house in Canada for Christmas, a time I will always cherish. My mother believed there was no greater good than giving to others, especially at holidays. So the Christmas House is really an expression of everything I learned about Christmas from her. My thoughts about that time pulled me through polio and gave me the strength to keep trying, even when I felt like giving up. I wanted people to know what Christmas is really about, that it is a time of love, sharing, and being grateful."

Before the guests departed, everyone promised to pitch in on the next Christmas House, whenever and wherever that may be. Later that evening, George sat alone and slowly turned the pages of the scrapbook again, savoring the memories each picture brought back. Albert quietly entered the garage and solemnly handed him a small envelope. He said, "Good night, son. I'm proud of you," and retired to his bedroom. George sensed that something very important was inside the envelope. He opened it and found a small snapshot of a young boy with a woman who appeared to be the boy's mother. On closer inspection, George recognized the boy as himself and the woman as his mother, Alice.

Alice Woodcock Skinner with her firstborn child, George, 1915

The picture was of the two of them alone taken before they were forever separated, and he realized that his father had saved it for all these years. George opened the scrapbook to the first page and placed the image next to a postcard of the Christmas House. He closed the scrapbook and held it to his chest.

Chapter 9 ~ Love Walks In

One of George's duties as sound engineer was recording actors auditioning for roles on Edward Bennett's radio broadcasts. He had to manually place the stylus, or needle, on an oversize recording disc the moment the director said, "Action." George performed his job meticulously because he knew the importance of a quality recording. It determined which voice actor got the job and, consequently, the quality and success of the entire show. He loved watching and listening to the actors' auditions. He never realized how many nuances and inflections the vocal cords were capable of. After work, on the streetcar ride home, he often entertained himself and others by practicing his own vocal skills on strangers, one day assuming the voice of an Oxford professor and the next the drawl of a southern gentleman.

On a particularly busy day in February 1939, Mr. Bennett entrusted George with recording the voice actors who were auditioning for his new show. The eighteen voice actors would read their parts when they were cued by the director, and George had to stop and start the recording for each new voice. When he was

Photo taken of George for his radio announcer's portfolio, 1939

recording an actual radio show for broadcast, he only had to drop the stylus at the beginning of the show and stop it at the end, listening for any problems that might occur during the recording. At those times, George could sit back and enjoy the actors' performances, but today he couldn't for fear of missing a cue from the director. When one female voice actor began speaking into the microphone, he looked up because he recognized her voice from somewhere.

"Good evening, ladies and gentlemen," she said cheerfully, "and welcome to Edward Bennett's Radio Theatre, brought to you by…" She continued reciting her lines while George scanned his memory for how he knew her. Suddenly, he realized she was the nurse's aide who had helped him compose the letter to First Lady Eleanor Roosevelt. She was strikingly beautiful in a slim red skirt, a white silk blouse, and high-heeled pumps. George couldn't take his eyes off her.

His stare made her nervous, and at first she cast a disgruntled glance at what she thought was a very rude soundman. As she continued speaking, her eyes locked on George's and she nearly flubbed her lines. Somehow she got through the audition, but when the director said, "Cut! Thank you. Next!" she didn't even hear it. She stood on stage transfixed, staring at George through the glass of the sound room. As she

Publicity photo of actress Pearl Theresa Majoros from her portfolio, 1939

watched him continue with his work, she thought about how their paths crossed at the oddest and most dramatic moments, first at the hospital, then right before his house burned down, and now at an important audition for her. She remembered how she had left a note for him before the fire. She had been disappointed that he never called but then decided not to bother him again. She had read in the newspaper that they were busy rebuilding and thought that with so much on his mind, he had probably forgotten all about the note.

George asked the director for a five-minute break. He came down on to the stage and gave Pearl an impulsive hug, which immediately broke the ice. Pearl

Pearl and George photographed at Edward Bennett's School of Radio, 1939

George and Albert pose by their Christmas tree in their living room

George and Pearl on their way to a date at a nightclub, 1939

excitedly told him about the note she had left for him before returning to San Francisco. Since he had never called, she had assumed he wasn't interested in talking to her. George was amazed; as she talked, he couldn't believe she was the same shy nurse's aide who had assisted him during his near-death experience. Then he realized that she also was the same woman who had waved to him in front of the Christmas House the night it caught fire.

He told her that he had never seen the note, that perhaps it had gone up in flames with the rest of the house. They laughed at the coincidence of their running into each other again at a recording studio. "Magical" is how they later described their encounters, as if fate had intended them to be together.

The director called everyone back to work, and George and Pearl quickly made a date to have dinner on Friday evening. Later that night, George couldn't recall anything that had happened that day except for meeting Pearl. The other auditions, his lunch hour, and the streetcar ride home were a big blur.

For the next few months, George and Pearl were inseparable. They could be seen at famous Hollywood nightclubs: cocktails at the Coconut Grove, dinner and a show at Earl Carroll's Theater, and movies at Grauman's Chinese Theatre. George told his father he

Souvenir photograph folders from the nightclubs frequented by Pearl and George, 1939 through 1942

George's first Christmas card
to Pearl, December 1939

Photo booth portrait of Pearl
and George, 1939

Inscription from George to Pearl,
1939

had found the girl of his dreams. She was exactly what he had hoped for all these years. Since Allison had broken it off with him, he had thought that finding another woman to love might be impossible, and now he couldn't be happier. It didn't matter if they were walking on the Santa Monica pier or listening to big band music at the Florentine Gardens; as long as Pearl was by his side, George was a happy man.

The holiday season of 1939 was an awkward time for George and Albert because there was no Christmas House. In fact, their only ode to Christmas that year was a single tree in the newly refurbished living room and one string of lights over the front porch. Yet out of habit they both often felt sudden urges to get up and turn on Christmas lights and adjust decorations.

That Christmas season, the magic in George's life was coming from Pearl, and he was glad he didn't have to spend his energy any other way. Father and son spent Christmas quietly at home with Pearl and a few close friends. On evening strolls, Pearl and George

noted that a few more houses than the year before
had Christmas decorations. It was a peaceful and joy-
ous Christmas for Pearl, George, and Albert. On New
Year's Day, George made a resolution to find a place of
his own, a home for Pearl and him.

≈

Pearl and George saw each other every day until Pearl
had to leave indefinitely for San Francisco to care for
her ailing father. George missed her terribly. By
November 1941, he couldn't stand it any longer. He
sent a telegram to Pearl, inviting her back to Hollywood for a romantic rendezvous the following
month. On December 23, she met him at the
Los Angeles train station, and he presented her
with a gardenia lei, which he had promised
her in the telegram, though he had mis-
spelled it as "leigh." The following evening, on
Christmas Eve, he proposed to her at the romantic
Florentine Gardens. She ecstatically accepted, and
they planned the wedding for the Christmas season of 1942. They agreed the ceremony should
boast a Christmas theme.

Pearl boarding a train bound
for San Francisco, 1941

George's love letter to Pearl,
December 6, 1939

Telegram George sent to Pearl
agreeing to meet her train, 1941

Pearl and George on the night they became engaged, celebrating with Albert and
Pearl's mother, Barbara Majoros, at the Florentine Gardens, December 1941

On the evening of December 23, 1942, George and Pearl were pronounced husband and wife at the Little Church of the Flowers in Glendale. The guests included the Christmas House gang, as well as neighbors, radio personalities, and old friends, and Pearl's father and mother traveled from San Francisco to attend. The wedding reception was held at the Knickerbocker Hotel in the heart of Hollywood. George and Albert decorated the reception hall in grand style with a few Christmas decorations from their garage. The colorful event, complete with a mariachi band, was a party never to be forgotten because George professionally recorded the festivities while acting as master of ceremonies. He interviewed and recorded his guests on transcription discs, which he later broadcast on his local radio show, "Hank the Night Watchman," on KGFJ.

Their honeymoon suite was a new apartment they rented on Shatto Place in Hollywood. On the way to the apartment in a hired car, the driver took a circuitous route and George questioned his navigational skills. He told the newlyweds that he thought they would like to see all the holiday decorations before the evening ended. From the flatlands to the hills above Hollywood, the town was ablaze with Christmas lights and holiday decor. Pearl winked at George and said, "Gee, I wonder where they got that idea?" George held her hand and smiled as they drove past house after house bedecked with Christmas decorations ranging from modest to extravagant.

George and his "Christmas angel" celebrating their first anniversary in their apartment on Shatto Place, December 23, 1943

Chapter 10 ~ The Visitor

In the spring of 1950, Albert helped George and Pearl with the down payment on a modest craftsman bungalow on Curson Avenue in the heart of Hollywood, only a half-block walk to either Sunset or Hollywood Boulevard. Frequently they spotted movie stars, such as Lauren Bacall, Clark Gable, or Marilyn Monroe, driving by in chauffeured limousines or dining in popular restaurants like Musso and Frank's. It was an exciting place to live in the late forties and early fifties. George and Pearl made a striking couple, and tourists often mistook them for movie stars. They were accustomed to posing for photographs and signing the autograph book with the name of whatever celebrity the tourists mistook them for.

George rode the bus to his new job as sound engineer at Capitol Records, and Pearl walked to her job as an executive secretary at the distinguished architectural firm Daniel, Mann, and Johnson. They usually spent weekends in the backyard at home, where George tended to thirty gorgeous rosebushes. Pearl kept busy with an outdoor aviary, where she bred

Pearl and George admire the garden in front of their home in Hollywood, 1950

Albert holding cat by the deteriorating waterwheel in the backyard, Mathews Street, 1949

Pearl's inscription to George on a Christmas card dated 1941

Pearl's Christmas card to George, 1941

dozens of parakeets. The backyard was a virtual Garden of Eden, full of the scent of roses and the songs of birds.

Albert's lady friend, Ruth Scott, moved into his house on Mathews Street, which was now fully restored. Few signs of the once-famous Christmas House remained, as weeds hid the path to the castle that had long since collapsed, and the wishing well was crumbling badly. Albert visited George and Pearl on weekends and helped with his son's household projects. Afterward, they would lie in hammocks and concoct elaborate plans to upgrade the house.

It was only a matter of time before a new version of the Christmas House at George and Pearl's became the main topic of discussion. Pearl wholeheartedly agreed with the idea, and by the fall of 1951 the trio began constructing new displays. A few remaining members of the original elf gang helped, too. Albert handled complex and physically challenging projects, and George acted as purchasing agent and public relations man. It was just like the old days, with father and son turning far-fetched fantasies into reality. "Yeah, we could do that" and "Why not?" were common phrases heard around the house that fall. Pearl added artistic touches to several projects. She painted life-size figures of Snow White and the seven dwarfs.

Pearl and George painting decorations for their house on Curson Avenue, November 1951

For the Skinners, Snow White somehow fit right in naturally next to Santa Claus, the reindeer, and the fake snow.

Many households, from the San Fernando Valley to the exclusive neighborhoods of the Beverly and Hollywood Hills, hired special effects companies and artists to create virtual movie sets of their homes, trying to outdo one another's Christmas displays. These elaborate displays didn't compare with the old-fashioned, homespun charm of the Skinner decorations. Maybe it was the sincere Christmas spirit that emanated from the Skinner home that attracted so much attention and adoration. When the new Christmas House opened for visitors, hundreds of people came from miles around, and news reporters covered the event, just as they had done before.

George stands in front of the house on Curson Avenue decorated for Christmas, 1953

George and Pearl waited until Christmas Eve to announce to Albert that next summer he would become a grandfather. Seven months later, in July of 1952, George and Pearl welcomed a healthy baby girl into the world, Georja Ann. Albert was as proud as a peacock, and he doted over his first grandchild.

When he realized George and Pearl could handle parenting without his assistance, he and Ruth took a long-overdue vacation. By train, they visited Yosemite National Park in central California, Mount Hood in Oregon, and the Rocky Mountains of Colorado. Albert wore warm-weather attire the entire time, no matter how low the temperature dropped. They crossed the border into Canada on the last leg of their trip.

In Hamilton, Ontario, his former hometown,

Albert stopped by an optician's office. His clothing gave him away as a tourist, and an odd one at that. He asked the clerk at the counter if the proprietor was in, and moments later the owner appeared from a back room. Albert asked him to adjust his ill-fitting eyeglasses. "No trouble at all. I'll be right back," the man said.

When he returned with the glasses, Albert tried them on and they fit perfectly.

"How much do I owe you?" he asked.

"No charge," replied the proprietor.

"Thanks. That's very nice of you," Albert said. Then he asked, "Do you mind if I take your picture?" The owner obliged, figuring the guy must be from California. Albert snapped the picture and thanked the man again for the excellent service.

The next day Albert returned to the shop and the owner wasn't quite so friendly this time. "What is it now, another picture? I'm really too busy for this," the man said gruffly.

"Do you think it strange that I took your photo yesterday?" Albert asked.

"Well, yes, but nothing you tourists do surprises me anymore."

Albert slid a card across the countertop to the shopkeeper. The man glanced at the card, which was a birth announcement from George and Pearl Skinner. "What on earth is this?" he asked. Then, as he read the name "George Skinner," a bell rang in his head. He read the card again and then looked up, carefully

Pearl and George with their young daughter, Georja, 1956

studying the features of Albert's face. He vaguely recognized the pale blue eyes, the large nose, and the uneasy smile. And then it started to sink in. After an awkward silence, the man said haltingly, "You wouldn't be my father, would you?"

Albert smiled and said nervously, "Yes, Gordon. I am."

Gordon Skinner standing in front of Skinner Opticians on John Street North and at his optician's workbench in Hamilton, Ontario, 1952

Gordon Skinner with his father, Albert, at Niagra Falls, Canada, 1952

Walter Skinner with his father, Albert, Hamilton, Ontario, 1952

~

Sixteen years later, in December 1968, Gordon stared
out the window of the yellow taxi as the driver steered
slowly down Hollywood Boulevard. Ever since Albert
had returned to Canada and visited his son at his optician's shop, George and Albert had been exchanging
letters with Gordon, catching up on all they had
missed in each other's lives. Over the years, their families grew, and the brothers wrote often about their
desire to see each other again, but the long train or air-
plane ride made it difficult, since neither could afford

Hollywood's residential districts are taking the shape of
wintry fairylands today as residents decorate their lawns
with elaborate Christmas settings. This is the colorful
decoration at the home of George Skinner, 1531 North
Curson avenue. Skinner, a former paralytic, and his wife,
Pearl, made the display themselves.

—Herald-Express Photo

*Los Angeles Evening Herald Express features
Curson Avenue house on front page, December
20, 1951*

*George demonstrates his recording work for a young
Georja as Albert watches, 1957*

the time away from work and family, and the ticket would have been an impossible expense. With Albert's help, Gordon had finally arranged to surprise his brother and meet his family, and he had told the driver about the excitement he felt.

As they drove through the streets of Los Angeles, Gordon was amazed at how different Californians were from people in Canada. The pedestrians looked like performers in a circus, with their flamboyant clothing, shirtsleeves, and other casual attire. The bright California sun gave everything a surreal glow. The palm trees looked prehistoric, people stared mysteriously at inlaid stars in a concrete sidewalk, and the architecture was a curious mix of old and new styles.

George, Albert, and Gordon Skinner, reunited after forty-eight years, in California, 1968

"Curson is the next street on the left. Are you ready?" the cabbie asked.

"I'm as ready as I'll ever be," Gordon said.

"Here it is." The cabbie stopped in front of the small bungalow, where two girls, a teenager and a ten-year-old, were stringing Christmas lights on the crooked picket fence around the front yard. Gordon could hear their animated conversation. The older girl said, "Get some more lights, Teresa. Go ask Grandpa for more. This simply won't do."

Just then George walked out on the front porch dressed as Santa Claus, his cane bedecked with white and red ribbon. Albert, high on a ladder, plugged in the huge tin star attached to the chimney. Gordon paid the driver and slowly approached the house.

"Merry Christmas! What can I do for you?" George shouted as the man crossed the street. He figured the fellow was a door-to-door salesman of vacuum cleaners or encyclopedias since he was dressed formally in an overcoat and a hat. As Gordon got closer, George stared at him, and wondered why he couldn't take his eyes off this man.

Gordon said, "Merry Christmas, brother."

George had never heard that one before, a salesman calling him "brother" just to get a foot in the door. And then he realized who this was. He couldn't believe his eyes. Gordon gave George a big bear hug, and the two men held each other as though their lives depended on it. Albert watched the encounter silently from the ladder. The two brothers embraced for minutes on end. When they finally separated, George said, "I can't believe it."

"As I live and breathe," Gordon said. "It's been a long time, George."

"Girls, I want you to meet

Teresa, Pearl, George, Albert, and Gordon in front of the Curson Avenue house, 1968

your uncle," George said, and Georja and Teresa ran over and eagerly hugged their Uncle Gordon. The children had lots of questions for the first uncle they had ever met. "Is it cold in Canada?" Georja asked. "You look just like my dad," Teresa chimed in.

Pearl greeted Gordon with a hug and welcomed him into their home. She took his coat, sat him down on the sofa, and set a large wooden scrapbook on his lap. George took a seat next to Gordon and put his arm around his younger brother. "There's a lot we have to catch up on," George said. "Welcome to the Christmas House."

Epilogue ~ The Power of a Dream

After years of separation, George and Gordon Skinner were finally together again. They formed a lasting friendship in the ten years that followed that first reunion. Their other brother, Walter, corresponded occasionally with George, though neither of them traveled to visit each other. And in the end, Albert was absolved and forgiven by his family.

The power of forgiveness and George's dream to see his brothers again brought about many miracles in his life, all except for one. George never saw or spoke to his mother again after he left Canada as a child. This left in George a melancholy that he carried with him for the rest of his life. Faithfully, each holiday season, he would hang a star on his rooftop in memory of the mother he barely knew.

My sister and I inherited that star, along with the crooked picket fence, the sleigh, and Snow White and the seven dwarfs. Every year, they come out of storage and are displayed during the balmy, 80-degree Christmas season on Maui, where we now live.

George, Albert, and Gordon enjoy a weekend in Las Vegas, 1969

Although the original Christmas House had been torn down, I often wondered if I could find visitors who had seen it and ask them about the impact it had on their lives. My question was answered after I was interviewed about the Christmas House for an article that appeared in the *Los Angeles Times* on Christmas

George poses by the waterwheel at the Mathews Street house shortly before Albert moved, 1962

Day 2000. Soon after it was published, Dan and Marjorie Gillingham, who had lived in Boyle Heights during the years of the Christmas House, contacted me through their daughter Nancy. They wanted to share their memories and tell me how much the house had meant to them. I even got the chance to meet Dan's sister, Margaret Gillingham, shortly before she passed away. The Gillinghams, the Bakers, and other families from the neighborhood have since told me that visiting the house is one of their favorite Christmas memories.

An anxious father, climbing up the fire escape at 10 and 11 o'clock at night to sneak in food for nourishment.

Long dreadful anxious nights that seemed never to end — days that were too long in coming —

Then at last sweet release — still in casts and uncurable! I was sent home —.

Scene 4 — a miracle by 100 churchwomen —

George Skinner's notes outlining a screenplay based on his ordeal with polio

Each holiday, when I share the scrapbook with guests in my own home, I see how it continues to inspire. From these holiday gatherings, the notion of telling this tale to a wider audience emerged.

As I began writing down my memories and unraveling the past, I often had guidance from unexpected places. During a particularly difficult time I wondered if my struggles were a sign that I should reconsider sharing my family's secrets. A trip to our local storage unit provided a message that I had to fulfill this mission. Among old 78 rpm records I discovered several small pieces of paper that chronicled my father's ordeal. He himself had written the story, outlined in screenplay format, from losing his family to his bout with polio to the creation of his Christmas House. Although he never mentioned these notes to me during his lifetime, they seemed to suggest that all along he had wanted to share his experience with others. My father had found a way to urge me to tell this story.

My hope is that the story of the Christmas House might help others find a way to hold on to and strive for whatever they believe in, no matter how impossible their goals might seem. George Skinner managed to focus his whole being on the possibilities rather than the seemingly insurmountable obstacles he faced. As George often said, "Dream big. Otherwise, why bother?"

Los Angeles Times

Southern California
Living

A woman wonders what lured thousands of yule visitors to her father's house in the 1930s. E2

Comics   E4, 5, 6

Kids' Reading page   E7

ROBERT GAUTHIER / L.A. Times

Reaching Into the Past

The shadow of Georja Skinner's hands frames a photograph of her father's house, at 919 S. Mathews St., decorated for Christmas in 1938.

ROBERT GAUTHIER / Los Angeles Times

There was something special about the Skinner Christmas House. It's gone now, but a daughter is hoping to uncover the secrets of its allure.

Something about that bungalow in Boyle Heights must have captured Christmas in the mid-1930s. Georja Skinner figures. Maybe it was the charm of a tiny house, with its white picket fence and inviting front porch, prettied up for the holidays. Or maybe it was the heart of the young man behind it, her late father, who then was recuperating from polio. Or, what neither it, wonders Skinner, 48, that drew tens of thousands of people to what became known as the Christmas House each

He and his father had no money for decorations at a time in which most neighbors could not even afford to string outside lights. So George Skinner relied on simple joys, like spinning Nat King Cole's scratchy Christmas records on a 78-rpm player in the living room while visitors filed through, and on clever ideas like the one to freeze steam to make icicles for the rooftop. (The record is fuzzy on exactly how that was done.)

He persuaded neighbors, movie studio executives and business owners to give time or donations, even the Los Angeles

The Los Angeles Times once again featured the Christmas House on December 25, 2000

Acknowledgments

At Hawaiian celebrations, a chant, or "'oli," is performed to ask ancestors to come forward and bless the gathering. In honoring this tradition, I have many generations of Skinners and Majoroses, as well as a large extended family, to thank for believing in my dream of bringing this story to others.

First and foremost, to my father, George, whose "never give up" attitude is ingrained in my genes: thanks to you I will always believe. Your humor and grace have carried me through my own life challenges. You are with me always in heart and deed.

To my mother, Pearl, whose love was beyond measure: you are as close as the scent of gardenias after a gentle rain.

To my grandfather Albert, who survived so much in his ninety-five years: thank you for all the great times we shared. The images you thought to capture throughout your life made it possible, in the pages of this book, to experience another time.

To my amazing sister, Teresa, my partner in stitching together our family history: from wading through literally tons of paper, old photographic negatives, postcards, and letters, I think we've proven there is nothing we can't accomplish when we do it together — accompanied by a glass of quality champagne.

And especially to my Uncle Gordon, who endured a tough childhood to become a leader in his community and an award-winning weight lifter well into his eighties: Dad loved you dearly, and this book is for you and all the Skinners in Canada, especially the latest addition, Elliot Gordon. If luck is on my side, my next trip to Hamilton will help me reconnect with Walter's family, too.

This book wouldn't have been possible without the help and kindness of dozens of people. To my extended "family-by-intention" from Hawaii to Hollywood, who are always there for my sister and me, to "Peggy of Hollywood" Harr, the Reeses, the Meltons, the Yonenakas, the Aveiros, and the Williams family, especially my best friend, Greg, and his incredible father, Dino: your support over the years has made it possible for me to fulfill my dream. I couldn't have done this without you. To the Curson Avenue "gang," the Roses, the Wexlers: what great times we've shared.

Special thanks to Kenneth Harris Sr, Lalita Tademy, Stefanie Powers, Frank Darabont, Michael Sloane, Richard Paul Evans, John Saul, Michael Sack, Renee Sakura, Governor Linda Lingle, Michael Mount, Mort and Natalie Lachman, Wendy Apple, B. G. Dilworth, Laurie Liss, Rita Rosenkranz, Susan Crawford, James Mylenek Sr., Tom Sewell, Alan Usler, Bill and Joelma Glassman, and my agents, Pat Quinn and Lane Zachary, whose enthusiasm and guidance have made all the difference in the world.

To New World Library's incredible editorial director, Georgia Hughes, who saw from the beginning a seed of promise in a story that "wouldn't let her go": your vision and heartfelt support has fueled me to do my best work. To all the team at New World, including publisher, Marc Allen; Mary Ann Casler and Tona Pearce Myers for their artistry and patience; and Eric Bolt, editor extraordinaire, who spent long hours with me revisiting my father's world: thank you for your dedication to this work.

To John and Shannon Tullius, directors of the Maui Writers Conference: you opened the door for a new writer to find her way through the literary labyrinth. Thanks to the conference I met my editor and my agents and landed a publisher. You are a godsend to every emerging writer who dares to walk this path.

A round of applause to graphic artist Terrie Eliker, who scanned the entire scrapbook before it crumbled altogether, and to Ada Yonenaka, whose first brutal edit of my book proposal prepared me for the journey ahead: you were right all along — less is more.

To the Skinner cat family, especially Miss Garbo: thanks for helping me each step of the way, with paw prints on my first drafts to prove it.

To all of George's fellow patients in Los Angeles County General Hospital and to those afflicted with paralysis and post-polio syndrome today: I hope this book brings a bright spot to your lives. Thanks to the thousands of medical professionals who worked to find a cure for polio, principally Dr. Jonas Salk. Special thanks to the members of the March of Dimes Foundation who worked in the early days for treatments and cures and who continue today to help save and repair lives. To the Roosevelt Warm Springs Institute, Rotary International and their Polio Plus Program, and the Christopher Reeve Paralysis Foundation: thank you for your global efforts to ensure that polio and paralysis will someday become afflictions of the past.

To Preston Goddard, Dick Whittington, Ione Judd, Bob Baker, and all the neighbors and church friends from Boyle Heights: thanks for being part of the Christmas House legacy. Special thanks to the Gillingham family, Dan, Marjorie, Nancy, and Margaret: meeting you in 2001, sixty-five years after you visited Dad's Christmas House, was beyond my wildest dreams.

And to my dear Lloyd, who keeps me humble and focused and who convinced me it was better to take the path of the unknown writer than to sit on the sidelines and wished I had: for your love and constant support I am forever grateful. To everyone who still believes in the magic of Christmas and keeps the spirit of the original Christmas House alive each holiday season: thank you for continuing the legacy.

And finally, to Alice, the grandmother I never knew: this book somehow has always felt like your idea. Through your images and in the telling of this story I have come to know you better. I hold you close to my heart and know that each Christmas your star still shines brightly.

Photo Credits and Permissions Acknowledgments

Every effort has been made to trace the ownership of all copyrighted material included in this volume. Any errors that may have occurred are inadvertent and will be corrected in subsequent editions, provided notification is sent to the publisher. Grateful acknowledgment is made to the following publishers and organizations who have generously granted permission to use quotations and/or photographs.

The photographs appearing on pages xi (and title page), 40, 42, 47 (2 photographs), 48 (2 photographs), 49 (left and photograph appearing in the *Gas News* article) 50 (2 photographs), 53, 54, 58, 60 (2 photographs), 61, 62, 64, 67 and the removable sticker on the back cover are by "Dick" Whittington and are used courtesy of "Dick" Whittington Photography, Los Angeles.

Photograph of iron lung appearing on page 7 from the cover of *Polio Chronicle*, 1933, courtesy of Roosevelt Institute archive.

Quotation from President Roosevelt's *Fireside Chats* and excerpt of letter from Eleanor Roosevelt courtesy of the Franklin Delano Roosevelt Presidential Library and Museum.

Articles and photographs reproduced on pages 41, 69 (right), 72, 89, and 93 courtesy of *Los Angeles Herald Express* Collection, Los Angeles Public Library.

Articles reproduced on pages 43, 54, 59, 73, and 74 courtesy of *Los Angeles Examiner.*

Article reproduced on page 45, "Front page of the *Los Angeles Times,*" published December 21, 1936 © 1936 Los Angeles Times. Reprinted with permission.

Article reproduced on page 49 courtesy of Southern California Gas Company *Gas News.*

Article reproduced on page 52 courtesy of *East Side Journal,* Los Angeles.

About the Author

$\mathcal{G}$eorja Skinner is a native of Hollywood, California, and president of Skinner Entertainment, a management and production firm with offices in Hawaii and North Hollywood. She was the first female sound mixer in network television on shows such as *All in the Family* and *The Jeffersons,* and she was nominated for an Emmy Award in 1977 and 1978 for tape-sound mixing. Skinner is currently on the "twenty-fifth year of her three-week vacation" in Hawaii. She established Maui's first film office in 1994 and prior to that time, she established and ran a successful public relations firm from 1983 until 1990, when her company was acquired by WPP Group's Hill and Knowlton-Communications Pacific.

Skinner currently resides in Napili, Maui. She considers the culture and beauty of Hawaii to be an integral part of her creative process. Skinner's next project is a documentary based on *The Christmas House* story.

Resources about Paralysis

The author wishes to thank the following organizations who continue to search for a cure and improve the quality of life for those living with paralysis and spinal cord injuries.

The Christopher Reeve Paralysis Foundation (CRPF) is committed to funding research that develops treatments and cures for paralysis caused by spinal cord injury and other central nervous system disorders. The foundation also vigorously works to improve the quality of life for people living with disabilities through its grants program, Paralysis Resource Center, and advocacy efforts.

The Christopher and Dana Reeve Paralysis Resource Center (PRC) is a program of the Christopher Reeve Paralysis Foundation and is funded through a cooperative agreement with the Centers for Disease Control and Prevention (CDC). The PRC's focus is to provide information services for paralyzed persons, their families, and caregivers.

Christopher Reeve Paralysis Foundation
500 Morris Avenue
Springfield, NJ 07081
800-225-0292
973-379-2690
973-379-2691
www.ChristopherReeve.org

The Christopher and Dana Reeve
Paralysis Resource Center
636 Morris Turnpike, Suite 3A
Short Hills, NJ 07078
800-539-7309
973-467-8270
973-379-2690
www.paralysis.org • info@paralysis.org

President Franklin Delano Roosevelt, named by *Time* magazine "the foremost statesman and political leader" of the twentieth century, founded the Roosevelt Warm Springs Institute for Rehabilitation in 1927. For three-quarters of a century, the Roosevelt Institute has been empowering individuals with disabilities to achieve personal independence. This mission has led to the development of one of the nation's most comprehensive approaches to medical and vocational rehabilitation, and has given rise to internationally recognized specialty programs, extensive specialty services, and a constantly expanding culture of compassion and expertise.

Roosevelt Warm Springs Institute for Rehabilitation
P. O. Box 1000
Warm Springs, GA 31830
Phone: 706-655-5000
Fax: 706-655-5011
TTY: 706-655-5176
www.rooseveltrehab.org
rwsir.webmaster@dol.state.ga.us

Rotary International was founded in 1905 in Chicago, Illinois, and is the world's first and one of the largest nonprofit service organizations. It is comprised of 1.2 million members working in over 30,100 clubs in more than 160 countries. Rotary International's Polio-Plus program was launched in 1985 to immunize all the world's children against polio by the end of 2005, Rotary's centennial. Rotary is the volunteer arm of the global partnership dedicated to eradicating polio in cooperation with the national health ministries, the World Health Organization (WHO), UNICEF, and the United States Centers for Disease Control and Prevention (CDC).

Rotary International
One Rotary Center
1560 Sherman Avenue
Evanston, IL 60201
Phone: 847-866-3400
Fax: 847-329-4101
www.rotary.org
polioplus@rotaryintl.org

New World Library is dedicated to publishing books and other media that inspire and challenge us to improve the quality of our lives and the world.

We are a socially and environmentally aware company and we make every attempt to embody the ideals presented in our publications. We recognize that we have an ethical responsibility to our customers, our employees, and our planet. We serve our customers by creating the finest publications possible on personal growth, creativity, spirituality, wellness, and other areas of emerging importance. We serve our employees with generous benefits, significant profit sharing, and constant encouragement to pursue our most expansive dreams.

As members of the Green Press Initiative, we print an increasing number of books with soy-based ink on 100% postconsumer waste recycled paper. We also power our offices with solar energy and contribute to nonprofit organizations working to make the world a better place for us all.

Our products are available
in bookstores everywhere.
For our catalog, please contact:

New World Library
14 Pamaron Way
Novato, California 94949

Phone: 415-884-2100 or 800-972-6657
Catalog requests: Ext. 50
Orders: Ext. 52
Fax: 415-884-2199

E-mail: escort@newworldlibrary.com
Website: www.newworldlibrary.com